Charles Asbury Stephens

The Knockabout Club in the Tropics

The Adventures of a Party of Young Men in New Mexico, Mexico and Central

America

Charles Asbury Stephens

The Knockabout Club in the Tropics
The Adventures of a Party of Young Men in New Mexico, Mexico and Central America

ISBN/EAN: 9783337340537

Printed in Europe, USA, Canada, Australia, Japan

Cover: Foto ©Thomas Meinert / pixelio.de

More available books at **www.hansebooks.com**

THE
KNOCKABOUT CLUB
IN THE TROPICS.

THE ADVENTURES OF A PARTY OF YOUNG MEN IN
NEW MEXICO, MEXICO, AND CENTRAL AMERICA.

BY

C. A. STEPHENS,

AUTHOR OF "THE KNOCKABOUT CLUB ALONGSHORE," "THE YOUNG MOOSE-HUNTERS,"
"CAMPING OUT," ETC.

FULLY ILLUSTRATED.

BOSTON:
ESTES AND LAURIAT,
301-305 Washington Street.
1884

Copyright, 1883,
By Estes and Lauriat.

CONTENTS.

CHAPTER		PAGE
	When, Why, and Where	11
I.	In New Mexico	20
II.	El Paso	72
III.	Christmas Tide in New Orleans	88
IV.	In La Habana	96
V.	A Primitive Milk-cart	108
VI.	Carnival	128
VII.	On Board the "City of Merida"	144
VIII.	Harbor of Vera Cruz	152
IX.	About the City	164
X.	Overland Party	181
XI.	In Quest of Coal Mines	189
XII.	Santa Semana	202
XIII.	Another Synod	214
XIV.	Popocatapetl	231

LIST OF ILLUSTRATIONS.

	PAGE
A Memory of Mexico . . *Frontispiece*	
"Well, Gentlemen" (Parlor Car scene)	13
The Peaks of Los Vegas	23
A Ground Sweat	24
Santa Fe	25
On the Line of the Railroad . .	26
A Native	27
Ancient Mexican Vase	28
Pueblo Interior	29
A Mexican Cart	32
Pioneer Life	33
Pueblo of Taos	36
A New Mexican Hacienda . . .	39
Bats Going out	50
Right Hand Half of a Pipe of Peace,	55
Going up the Table-Lands . . .	59
Along the Bluff	63
Scene in New Mexico	67
"Sharles, pe careful vare you shoots!"	69
A Desert	78
Chihuahua	81
An Interior	84
Getting a Start	86
New Orleans	89
Mouth of the Mississippi River .	92
Jacksonville, Florida	93
St. Augustine	95

	PAGE
Havana	97
Avenues of Palms	101
Moses' Siesta	105
Cut of Fountain	109
Milk Cart	111
Havana	113
Scene in Cuba	117
Horses Bathing	119
Attempted Assassination	121
In Every Land	123
John Chinaman	124
Chinese at his Devotions	125
Relics of Columbus	126
Gathering Palms	129
Killing the Snake	133
A Tragic Incident	138
In the Wind and Water	142
Sea Eagles Fighting	147
Vera Cruz	149
View in Tierra Caliente	153
Beggar	155
Table-Land of Mexico	156
Hen-Coop	159
Calendar Stone	160
The Canal — Ruins of covered way to the Inquisition — San Cosme Aqueduct, City of Mexico . .	162
Popocatapetl	165
Virgin of Guadaloupe	167

LIST OF ILLUSTRATIONS.

	PAGE
Cathedral, Mexico	168
A Dangerous Adventure	171
Queretaro from the Hill of Bells	173
Maximilian — Carlotta	178
Death of Maximilian	180
Indian Hut	182
Church at Santiago	183
Young Ocelots	187
The Herd of Mountain Sheep	190
Silver Mine	191
Prospecting	193
In Mexico	195
Silver Country	198
Street Scene in Mexico	203
A Native Lady	205
Canal of La Viga, City of Mexico	206
Scene during Santa Semana	207
Spanish Beggar in Mexico	208
Spanish Grandee on His Way to the Fight	209
The Matador	212
Chapultepec	213
Castle of Chapultepec	217
Pyramid of Cholula	218
Ruins in Mexico	221
Mexican War God, Huitzelopochtli	223
Aztec Writing	224
Aztec Idol	225
Aztec Numbers	226
Mexican Priests of the Past	229
General Porfirio Diaz	230
Game of the Fliers	232
An Ancient Aztec Teocelli	234
Montezuma	236

THE KNOCKABOUT CLUB IN THE TROPICS.

WHEN, WHY, AND WHERE.

TIME: Nov. 19th, the season following the cruise of the "Knockabout Club Alongshore," to Greenland in June, and its return to Boston in September.

Place: Drawing-room car *Las Cruces*, Santa Fé Railroad, *en route* for the city of Mexico via Santa Fé, El Paso, and Chihuahua.

CENTURY.

The idea of combining study and travel in place of a mere book education, was first broached and put in practice by the Camping-Out Club in 1872.

YEAR.

MIDNIGHT.

Later, the Steamship College Association attempted it on a grander scale. The present Knockabout Club has been acting on the same idea now for two seasons past, as recorded in the two preceding volumes of this series of travels.

NIGHT.

The main points of the scheme will be readily apprehended from the following record of the proceedings of the club immediately on meeting for the trip, at La Junta, Colorado. For since some members of our fraternity hail from California and some from Massachusetts, this obscure little junction on the plains was the most convenient place of rendezvous for the tour of Mexico.

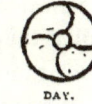
DAY.

From this point to El Paso, the exclusive use of the car had been secured by the party for seven days, if desired, it being our intention to see whatever was of interest in New Mexico first, and in Old Mexico later.

On this trip our hearts were gladdened by the presence of that former promoter and pioneer of the Steamship College idea, Mr. G. W. Burleigh, whom some of our readers may remember as "Wash." It was he who — by common acclamation — made the informal opening speech as soon as we were comfortably "fixed" in the *Las Cruces*.

"Well, gentlemen," said he, "here we are, and every man of you — if I know myself and can read your faces, knows what he is here for. It is to prove to the American public that our plan of getting an education is the correct one — prove it by ourselves as an illustration of it. That may not sound modest, if our scribe records it in his book, but it is business, nevertheless. So many theories are broached to the public every year that we cannot expect people to hail them all with transports of joy. It is only the theories that are *proved* to be *correct* which command attention. All great ideas, too, must have time to take root and grow in the public mind. It was so with railways; it was so with the telegraph; and it will be so with our new plan of education. Its utility and its superiority will have to be demonstrated before our people will accept it. Thus far the idea has had to push its own way to public notice. Ten years ago four boys (Raed, Wade, Wash, and Kit) set off afoot and alone to the Maine woods, studying and making notes on natural history, botany, and geology as they travelled. At night they camped out and cooked their own food. At the end of their tour they came back hale, hearty, and with the feeling that they had *taken in a good deal;* that they had learned more than if they had been in a college for the same time. Out of this experience, in time, grew the project for a steamship college, — a "college" that should combine travel and study in the most world-wide sense. They worked at this idea and tried to raise the necessary million of dollars to fit out a steamship. But the time was unfortunately chosen. The commercial panic of 1873–74 paralyzed everything. The enterprise came to a standstill; and the Woodruff

"WELL, GENTLEMEN, HERE WE ARE."

expedition, — an imitation of the Steamship College plan, — which meant well, but was badly managed, gave the public an erroneous impression of our undertaking, which by no means helped it forward.

"But a great idea will not die. You, gentlemen, took it up, and are, in a practical and common-sense way, putting it to test, and giving the public the net results of your experience. No better plan could have been chosen. You are doing wisely. Slowly but surely you will win public opinion to this mode of educating boys; and the boys of the next generation will thank you for it. The age of dull, dreary text-books is passing; a better method of teaching is coming in. You, gentlemen, are its pioneers.

"I know your plans and methods for this tour of Mexico, I think, but I shall be glad to hear them stated clearly."

In response, our Club president, Mr. Dearborn (whom former readers may remember as "Harold"), said: —

"Our plans are very simple. We have no constitution or by-laws. We are merely to keep our eyes open as we go, see all we can and make a note of all worth remembering, or which bids fair to be of any use to us in after-life. As we journey, different members of the Club will stop at different places for a few hours, or a day, in order that the whole ground may be covered and as many objects of interest seen as possible. Every evening, or every second or third evening, as most convenient, we are to confer and compare notes. Each one will then tell what he has seen and noted, so that mutually we may each get the benefit of what the whole Club has observed.

"Out of all this the *scribe* is to select what he deems the most interesting, which is to be published in book-form for the express purpose of interesting other young men and boys in our mode of education.

"As I have said, we have no fixed rules. In fact, I have stated about all there is to state by way of a *curriculum*. Briefly, it is to travel abroad, see everything worth seeing and *take it in*, so that it can always be of use."

"One thing more," Brett remarked. "It is a matter of secondary importance, perhaps; but it is one that has been several times sug-

gested and agreed on. Each one is advised to have at hand some really good book, some standard history, scientific work, or novel of the better class, to read at odd hours. This in addition to newspapers and magazines, which every one reads, of course, and which really form one of the best helps to education that the times afford."

"It has sometimes been talked, too," remarked Davis, (Moses O.) " that different members of the Club should direct their attention specially in different lines of observation. For example, Brother Stein has sometimes looked after the mineralogy and geology of a country, having a taste, personally, for those things. On the other hand, Forney, who has had the advantages of a West Point course of study, attends to the military matters and looks up the forts and soldiers. For a like reason, Mr. Garland, whose previous studies have been of a theological nature, makes a specialty of the churches, religion, and morals of the people. While Karzy attends to the pictures, statuary, and art matters generally; also makes pictures for the published account of the tour, and intends taking photographic views, if I rightly construe the purport of that little portable camera which adorns his hips at odd hours. In this way a profitable division of labor, or rather of eyesight, is proportioned off; and the results thus far have been, to speak conventionally, of a highly satisfactory character. In other words, it works well."

"Yes, it works well in Moses' opinion," Karzy observed. "For in the way he has divided the *labor of eyesight*, you will observe that he has taken no share to himself. That suits Moses."

"If I have arrogated no part of this responsibility to myself it is from my modesty, I am sure," insisted Moses. "Besides, I have a share and a heavy one; I have the whole Club to look out for. I have to labor with railway conductors and intimidate sleepy car-porters and hotel-clerks. I have to get bargains in cars, and, generally speaking, stand between the great, hard-fisted world and my more ethereally minded fellow-clubsmen. Why, I hired this car for seventy dollars when our worthy president was just going to pay a hundred and ten. I got 'circus rates' for the whole Club, when our friend, the scribe, was just on the point of paying regular fare. Same thing at the hotels, too. Do you call that no *share*, my boy? Why, my dear fellow, if you were to let these Western railroads and hotels have their own sweet will with us we should reach the far-famed city of the Montezumas only to enter a third-class poor-house, if they have them. Without arrogance, as I said, I deem myself the financial backstay of the whole Club. It is my business to see that nobody beats us, and, well, to beat the other side as much as is consistent with the dignity of the Club. I've got a gauge on that. It is my sphere to level all obstacles which get in our way. In fact, to use a railroad term, I'm the cow-catcher of this party; and I don't spare myself. For instance, at Denver, where I obtained 'circus rates' at the hotel there for the party, the clerk had the impudence to ask me if I were the clown. Now, in all fairness, I judged that to be a joke and a too personal one to let him get away with and still command his highest respect, which I was bound to have, of course. I took time. I looked him all over, his diamond pin and all; then I reached over slowly and putting my hand confidentially on his shoulder, drew him over toward me, with an amount of physical power which I think our friend Stein here would have estimated at three hundred foot-pounds. I fairly raised him on to the register and whispered in his ear, "Yes, marm, I'm just that, and if you are not satisfied about me, I will give you (here I put about three hundred foot-pounds more) a perfectly satisfactory guarantee.'

"'All right! all right!' said he. That's all right!' and I eased him back. You see how I have to work."

"Yes," said Harold, "Moses is all he claims to be, ay, more. He is more than the backstay he is the backbone, and a big one. But there is another matter. When we first began our series of trips and tours, we were nicknamed the Knockabout Club by outsiders, who only partially comprehended our motives for travel. That name stuck to us and we adopted it. But there are certain members who objected to the name, as sounding too rough-and-tumble, and as calculated to give the public an erroneous idea of our scheme of self-education. One member wishes the Club to be rechristened as *The Athenian*

Club, because, he says, we are like the ancient Athenians, in that we are on the lookout constantly to hear or find out some new thing."

"I suggest in all seriousness, gentlemen, that we be called the Athenian Club," said Karzy. "I like that name far better."

Some discussion followed. Several other names were suggested. But the majority did not believe it worth the while to change the name. This sentiment was fairly well expressed by Moses O., who said:—

"Let folks call us what they like. If we are all right, fair, square, and honorable, and put our idea through, we shall make any name they choose to call us respectable. We are no *dilettantes*, anyhow. The Knockabout Club is a good enough name for us. It's like a stiff brown paper cover; it will wear well and won't show dirt. A nicer one, with ferns and lilies on it, might get soiled."

So the matter of the Club name was tabled for the present.

CHAPTER I.

IN NEW MEXICO. — ADOBE PEOPLE. — EL PASO. — THE CLUB IN SYNOD. — A GROUND SWEAT. — A CHINESE FUNERAL. — SANTE FÉ. — OLD SPANISH MINING. — TURQUOIS. — KARZY'S STORY OF TURLEY'S MILL. — IN A KANSAS PARLOR. A DROLL MINE. — MILLIONS OF THEM ? — INDIANS, BOYS, AND BATS. — A BEE STORY. — BEARS. — A SORELY TROUBLED DUTCHMAN.

FROM La Junta, five hours across the plains, and through the outlying spurs of the Rockies, brought us to the long tunnel (700 meters), where the railway pierces the "divide" and crosses the boundary between Colorado and New Mexico. Immediately we reached the flourishing new town of Raton (the word means *mouse*), situated in the midst of characteristic New-Mexican scenery: plains bounded all around by tall, saw-tooth peaks, now clad in snow. Snow, indeed, was seen lying to the depth of three and four inches on the ground beside the track. This was on the 19th of November. It must be borne in mind that New Mexico lies at an elevation of from five thousand to seven thousand feet above sealevel.

The Americans here are either miners and stock-raisers, or railway employees. There is, moreover, a kind of *ground* population of mongrel Mexicans who live in adobe huts, at scattered ranches and in old mission hamlets. The external characteristics of these indigines are squalor, stagnancy, and perennial small-pox. Once seen is seen enough. Of all the animal species which old Mother Earth has from time to time produced, the genus "Greaser" is about the dullest and most hopeless.

The larger New-Mexican towns — Las Vegas, Santa Fé, Albuquerque, Socorro — are at present in a curious state of transition from "Greaser" lethargy to West-American push and rush. Whether the "Greaser" can be waked up into a citizen is the standing problem in these parts just now. There are bets on it even. No one can quite say as yet. He looks very tired, very sleepy. It is, in truth, a tired race.

Karzy and Mr. Garland stopped off at Raton — to explore. Moses, Harold, "Wash," and the scribe left the car at Las Vegas and went up to the hot-springs, distant six miles. These hot sulphur springs are becoming within the last two years a notable resort for invalids. But our party went merely to see the place and get a good dinner at its really fine hotel. A good dinner and a comfortable hotel are not yet so common in New Mexico as to be objects of indifference. Stein, Brett, and Forney continued on to Santa Fé and Albuquerque; and it was not till the twenty-fourth of the month, five days after, that we all met again, at El Paso, on the frontier.

El Paso, situated as it is at the gateway of travel and trade into Mexico, will no doubt be one of the leading cities of the Southwest in the not distant future. But it is located in a terribly dreary region, a desert, which stretches east and west from Middle Texas to Fort Yuma. Little or no rain, a pitiless summer sun, and dust blizzards, so dense that a man may get lost in his own door-yard, are the climatic features.

As the car was still at our service, we thought it as well to lodge in it and have our food brought from a restaurant. It was on the car, therefore, that we had our first dinner together, and then proceeded to compare notes and tell what each had seen and heard in New Mexico.

Harold, acting as chairman for the time, opened the "synod" by asking Moses O. what he knew; "What do you know to-day, Moses?" was his question.

"I demur to such a question," Moses objected, "because it carries the injurious insinuation that I possibly do not know anything."

"True," said Harold, "very properly objected. Well, then, what have you seen?"

"I've seen a man take a *ground sweat*," replied Moses.

"A *ground sweat!* That sounds serious," Brett said.

"Not very serious; on the contrary, it was rather laughable," said Moses; whereupon he discoursed to us as follows on the subject: —

A GROUND SWEAT.

Now and then we hear of a sick person who, seized by some instinctive impulse, has had himself buried to the chin in the ground; and either from the corrective properties resident in the bosom of Mother Earth, or from the energetic action of his faith, a cure has followed on the whim.

The earth, meaning the fresh, clean ground, is undoubtedly surcharged with electric and vital forces, since all forms of life are seen to rise from its surface.

At Las Vegas we witnessed a more practical and systematic application of the ground-cure idea. Here at the foot of the mountains, on the south banks of the Rio Gallinas, are numerous hot sulphur springs, where from time immemorial the Mexican people had been wont to bathe for various diseases. An extensive bathhouse has been erected within the past year, into which the hot water from the various springs, to the number of eighteen or twenty, is brought, and the accommodations greatly enlarged for taking both tub and vapor baths, for the purification of diseased organisms.

The earth below the springs through which the mineral waters trickled down to the river has been found to be very strongly impregnated with these chemical elements, which the water brings up from deep in the earth. Of late, the idea of giving invalids a "ground sweat," so to speak, in this chemically strong earth, has entered the minds of physicians, and been put in practice, with good results, it is alleged.

THE PEAKS OF LAS VEGAS.

On the day of our visit the bath-house, or rather the bath-shed, presented a truly singular spectacle. Four long, deep bath-troughs of deal planks were here set in a row. Each was filled to the brim with black mud of the consistency of thick treacle, and of a temperature of from ninety-eight to one hundred and six degrees. At the hour when we entered the shed each of the troughs had at one end what looked to be a human head set on a little brown rubber pillow.

And they were heads! Immediately they began to smile, then to talk. Nor were they dissevered heads. The bodies to which they belonged were simply down in the black mud out of sight. The heat can be increased to as hot as the person can bear. A strong odor of sulphur emanates from the mud; and on the whole the association of ideas and odors was hardly pleasant, and had a purgatorial suggestion. Yet for persons in *limbo* the bathers

A GROUND SWEAT.

seemed quite merry; they talked, joked, laughed. Often they remain in the mud for an hour or more, and come out in a somewhat parboiled condition, but much regenerated physically, as they seemed to think. The superintendent told us of several apparently wonderful cures; and if ever any of you are so unfortunate as to be troubled with ailments of an obscure nature, I should be inclined to advise a ground sweat.

"We will think of it," said Harold.

"Santa Fé is really a rather interesting old town," said Stein. "It is the second oldest town in the United States, I believe, if not the first. Before the building of railroads west of the Mississippi it was the headquarters and point of departure for all the wagon-trains, which then carried on the trade of the north Territories. In fact, our route down into New Mexico was along the old 'Santa Fé Trail,' or wagon-road.

"The Spaniards came up here from their then newly conquered vice-royalty of Mexico, as early as the middle of the sixteenth century. The Indian population

SANTE FÉ.

— of which the present Zunis and Pueblos are the feeble descendants — then numbered hundreds of thousands.

"The Spaniards set them all to work in the mines, getting out silver; and there is little doubt that the conquerors secured millions of dollars worth of this metal. These early miners knew nothing of the high explosives; they transported their ores on the backs of mules and men, hundreds of miles, to be smelted in the most primitive manner, yet wealth flowed into the lap of Spain in such profusion as to astonish all Christendom. At present, one miner can do as much work in a day as a score could have done two centuries ago in the same time.

"I visited an old turquoise mine near Santa Fé, where vast num-

ON THE LINE OF THE RAILROAD.

bers of these then precious gems were worked out. This old mine is in what the Indians called Mount Chalchuitl, which is the native name for turquoise.

"The rocks which form Mount Chalchuitl are distinguished from those of the surrounding and associated ranges by their white color and decomposed appearance, closely resembling tuff and kaolin, and living evidence to the observer, familiar with such phenomena, of extensive and profound alteration; due probably to the escape through them at this point of heated vapor of water, and perhaps of other vapors and gases, by the action of which the original crystalline structure of the mass has been completely decomposed or metamorphosed, with the production of new chemical compounds. Among these the turquoise is the most conspicuous and important. In this yellowish-white and kaolin-like tufaceous rock the turquoise is found in thin veinlets or little balls of concentrations called 'nuggets,' covered with a crust of nearly white tuff, which within consists generally as seen on a cross fracture of the less valued varieties of this gem, but occasionally afford fine sky-blue stones of higher value for ornamental purposes. Blue-green stains are seen in every direction among the decomposed rocks; but the turquoise in masses of any commercial value is extremely rare, and many tons of the rock may be broken without finding a single stone which a jeweller, or *virtuoso*, would value as a gem.

A NATIVE.

"One is deeply impressed, on inspecting this locality, with the enormous amount of labor which in ancient times has been expended here. The waste of *débris* excavated in the former workings cover an era of at least twenty acres. On the slopes and sides of the great piles of rubbish are growing large cedars and pines, the age of which — judging from their size and slowness of growth in this very dry region — must be reckoned by centuries. It is well known that in 1680 a large section of the mountain suddenly fell in from the undermining of the mass by the Indian miners, killing a considerable number; and it was this accident which caused the great rebellion of the Pueblos and the expulsion of the Spaniards in that year, two centuries since.

"The irregular openings in the mountain called 'wonder-caves' are the works of the old miners. It was this sharp slope of the mountain which fell. In these chambers, which have some extent of ramification, are found abundantly the fragments of ancient pottery, with a few entire vessels, some of them of curious workmanship, ornamented in the style of color so familiar in the Mexican pottery. Associated with these were numerous stone hammers, some to be held in the hand and others swung as sledges, fashioned with wedge-shaped edges and a groove for a handle. A hammer weighing over twenty pounds was found, to which the wyth was still attached, with its oak handle — the same scrub oak which is found growing abundantly on the hillsides — now quite well preserved after at least two centuries of entombment in this perfectly dry rock.

ANCIENT MEXICAN VASE.

"The stone used for these hammers is hard, tough hornblende.

INTERIOR OF A PUEBLO HOUSE.

With these rude tools and without iron or steel, using fire in place of explosives, these patient old workers managed to break down and remove the incredible masses of these tufaceous rocks which form the mounds already described.

"That considerable quantities of the turquoise were obtained can hardly be questioned. We know that the ancient Mexicans attached great value to this ornamental stone, as the Indians do to this day.

"The familiar tale of the gift of the large and costly turquoise by Montezuma to Cortez for the Spanish crown, as narrated by Clavigero in his history of Mexico, is evidence of its high estimation.

"It is not known that any other locality in America has furnished turquoise in any considerable quantity; the only other place being that Columbus district in Nevada discovered by Mr. J. E. Clayton, and is not yet worked.

"Chemically turquoise is a hydrous aluminum phosphate. Its blue color is due to a variable quantity of copper oxide, derived from associated rocks. It is found that the Cerrillos turquoise contains 3.81 per cent. of this metal, formula phosphoric acid 32.26, alumina 47.0, water 20.5."

"For your incidents and those facts which you have taken pains to make exact and scientific, we are greatly obliged, Stein," said Harold. "And now Karzy, what have you seen or heard, of interest?"

"I don't know that it will at all interest you; but I have heard and written out, at some length, the story of a New-Mexican pioneer who seems to have been a rather remarkable man, and whose fate was a sad one. But as I said, I fear you will find it but tiresome."

"Well, the proof of the pudding is in the eating," observed Moses. "Go ahead with your little story. Anything historic should be of some value."

Whereupon Karzy read an account of—

THE STORMING OF TURLEY'S MILL.

The stirring and often sanguinary annals of New Mexico, in her earlier days, contain nothing more thrilling, nor more apt to inspire pity and indignation, than the fate of one of her first American settlers, named Turley.

Turley settled in the Territory as early as 1837. He made his home not very far from Santa Fé, on a small river known as the Arroyo Hondo; and here,

A MEXICAN CART.

within a few years, he had by far the most flourishing rancho in the whole Taos district.

Herds of cattle, goats and sheep fed on the slopes of the Sierra. Innumerable hogs swarmed in his corrals; while broad, enclosed fields produced great crops of corn and wheat.

With true Yankee enterprise, Turley built a heavy dam on the Hondo, which gave him water-power for a large grist-mill, the only one in that section. In so remote a country everything had to be home-made, and Turley seems to have been a man of boundless ingenuity. He contrived looms and spinning-wheels as

STREET SCENE IN TAOS.

well as mill-stones. In fact, his rancho contained within its corrals all the industries of a town. All the things necessary to comfortable civilized life were made there, and made in profusion.

His wife was a Mexican; and the Americans in his employ had, many of them, also married Mexican wives. Rosy children, uniting the fair complexions of the Anglo-Saxon with the darker tint of their Mexican mothers, played along the Hondo, making its banks echo to their juvenile merriment.

Many Mexicans and Pueblo Indians worked for Turley, and were always so well fed and well paid, that a contest often arose among them for a chance to hire at the grand *rancho del Americano*.

Turley is still further mentioned as being one of the most jolly, good-natured fellows in existence; one of those big-hearted men who endear themselves to all about them, — hearty, bluff, manly souls, yet with the tender hearts of women.

His kindness and generosity were unlimited. No hungry Mexican or Comanche Indian (even when at war) was ever turned away from Turley's. He fed all alike, and treated every man who came to him, whether savage or civilized, as a brother. If a wanderer could but make his way to Arroyo Hondo he was sure of welcome and aid.

Such was Turley when the political difficulties between Texas and Mexico, which finally terminated in the Mexican war, broke out. All the American settlers of New Mexico were in jeopardy as to their lives and property. Turley, however, took no precautions, believing that the service he had rendered the people would be a sufficient safeguard, and deeming himself, indeed, a citizen of the country.

One morning in December, that year, a man named Otterbees, in Turley's employ, who had been sent to Santa Fé a few days before, suddenly made his appearance at the gate of the corral, and in great alarm announced that the Mexicans and Pueblo Indians had risen and massacred Governor Bent and all the other Americans in the place.

"And they are on their way here this very moment!" concluded Otterbees. "Fly for your lives!"

"Fly!" exclaimed Turley, contemptuously. "I'm a citizen of New Mexico. I've lived by its laws, and treated every man in it as if he were my own brother. They won't hurt me."

"You don't know them 'Greasers' yet!" cried Otterbees. "But you soon will!" he added, and spurring his horse galloped off.

But Turley would not believe in the danger; or if danger there were, he was resolved to stand by his property.

There were at that time nine Americans at the mill, — pioneers and hunters, — all dead shots. They closed the gates of the corral and prepared their arms.

None too quickly! For within less than two hours an uproar of wild shouts was heard, and immediately several hundred Mexicans and Indians made their appearance in the road, armed with guns, lances, bows and arrows. Among them were several Mexican officers.

Advancing to the gate, they shouted for Turley, who at once stepped forth and asked what was wanted.

"Give up the rancho and all the Americans in it," said an interpreter. "Your own life shall be spared, but every other American in Taos dies to-day."

PUEBLO OF TAOS.

"My own life!" shouted Turley in great anger. "Do you think I would give up my countrymen to have their throats cut?" Never! Do your worst; I'll fight you with my last breath!"

Then was seen the full extent of Mexican ingratitude. "*Maten los Tejanos! Maten los burros!* — Kill the Texans! Kill the jackasses!" was the cry.

The mill and other enclosed buildings lay at the foot of a gradual slope of the

Sierra, which was covered with cedar scrub. In front, about twenty five yards below the corral, ran the Hondo. The banks were steep and broken. In the rear was some garden ground, enclosed by lower fences. In this plat a wicket gate opened from the main corral.

The crowd of Indians and Mexicans surrounded the place on all sides, and keeping in cover of the cedar and broken ground opened a brisk fire of bullets and arrows whenever any one within the corral showed himself.

But the defenders, meantime, were not idle. If an Indian or a Mexican exposed himself in the scrub there whistled a ball from an unerring rifle, and within the first hour numbers of the attacking party were shot down. The windows of the mill and still-house were blocked with wheat in bags, leaving only loop-holes through which to fire. The stock of ammunition, however, was not large, there being but about sixty shots for each man.

The afternoon passed in this way and darkness set in. All night the nine Americans stood at their posts, watching every manœuvre of their enemies with grim determination. Firing went on by spells whenever one party caught sight of the other. Fresh props were set at the gates, and every window and door was barricaded still more strongly. Turley was everywhere, and his constant word was, "Cheer up, men! We may beat 'em off yet!"

In the morning it was found that the Mexicans had effected a lodgment in the horse-sheds, which stood a little apart from the other buildings, but one end of which adjoined the side of the mill. Protected by the shed, they were striving to break a hole through the wall of the mill.

But the great strength and thickness of the adobes and logs of which it was composed resisted their efforts completely. At length, finding their position in the shed of no use to them, they seemed anxious to get out of it.

To get out, now that it was light, however, they were obliged to cross an open space of a few yards, to gain cover of an angle of the corral fence. Two or three darted across unhurt. Then, the attention of the defenders being called to their ruse, a man named Albert covered the spot with his rifle; and the next one who started to run across was shot on the instant, and fell dead in the centre of the open space.

It chanced to be a Pueblo chief, and immediately one of his followers dashed out and attempted to drag the body away. Again Albert's rifle poured forth its deadly contents on the instant, and the Indian, struck to the heart, fell upon the body of his expiring chief.

Nothing daunted, however, another rushed out, and still another; but both fell, mortally wounded, under the unerring aim of the pioneers.

After a pause of a few moments, three Indians darted out together, and seizing their chief by the arms and head, had lifted the body off the ground, when three puffs of smoke blew from the barricaded windows of the mill, followed by the loud cracks of as many rifles. The three daring Pueblos leaped wildly into the air, and fell upon the ghastly heap which already encumbered the little open plat.

Up to this time the defenders had suffered no loss. As if maddened by this exhibition of marksmanship, both Indians and Mexicans raised a yell, and rushing forth from their coverts, ran up close to the mill, all firing at once.

Eight or nine of them were shot; but two of the Americans were mortally wounded at the same instant. One died in a few minutes; but the other, who was shot through the lower part of the body, suffered great agony.

They bore him into the still-house and laid in a large bin of wheat, that being the softest couch to be found. All day he lay there, moaning piteously; for the remaining seven did not dare to leave their posts to attend him.

About midday the attack was renewed more fiercely than before, the Indians having grown furious from so many baffled attempts, and the loss of so many of their warriors. The little garrison withstood it bravely, never wasting a shot, but firing coolly and only when a fair mark was presented to their certain aim.

Not more than ten shots now remained to them, however; and to add to the danger of their situation the Indians succeeded in firing the roof of the mill with blazing arrows. It flamed up fiercely and bade fair to involve the whole rancho in destruction.

But at this juncture Turley hoisted the gates of the sluice, letting water into the basement, and with the aid of buckets they partially extinguished the fire. Coals and blazing brands fell about them, however; and fire was constantly breaking out from this cause in the lower part of the mill, which was only put out by vigorous efforts.

While thus employed the assailants battered a gap in the corral, and in their blind fury shot and speared the hogs and cattle, which had been shut up since the day before. A few volleys drove them back again; but these reduced the ammunition of the Americans to three or four rounds.

A successful defence through another night being now hopeless, they held council, and agreed that as soon as darkness fell, each man should attempt to cut his way out as best he could and take to the Sierra as a last chance.

Acting on this plan, Albert and another man, just at dusk, dashed out at the wicket-gate that opened into the garden, firing their rifles full in the faces of the Mexicans. In the confusion Albert threw himself under the log fence, among high weeds. While lying there unobserved he saw his comrade shot down but a few steps off.

A MEXICAN HACIENDA.

Crouching motionless under the fence till the darkness had deepened, Albert was able to creep unnoticed into the cedar scrub, and thus he gained the Sierra. Two days later he reached the American settlement on the Greenhorn, nearly dead with thirst and fatigue.

Turley himself made his way out through the sluice of the mill, and keeping under water all but his head, went some distance up the Hondo. The next morning, as he was following a trail some miles to the northward, he met a mounted Mexican whom he had often befriended, named Lorando. This man had but recently spent a fortnight at the mill on a visit to Turley.

Thinking he might confide in the Mexican, Turley told what had occurred. "You see what a strait I'm in, Lorando," said he. "Let me have your horse. Here is my gold watch. I'll swap with you."

With a perfidy worthy of Judas, Lorando professed friendship, but refused to give Turley the horse, on the plea that he might be found out by so doing. But he told Turley to hide during the day at a deserted rancho near by, and that the following night he would come to him with food and a mule.

This Turley was induced to do, for he supposed that he had bound Lorando to him by so many benefits that he could not find it in his heart to doubt him.

Lorando rode straight to the mill, which the Mexicans were now plundering, and informed them of Turley's whereabouts.

As soon as night came thirty of the inhuman wretches, with Lorando at their head, rode to the place where Turley was concealed. Stationing the gang about the yard, Lorando went to the door and called to the American. On the unfortunate man's coming out, they fired on him and he fell, stricken with a score of balls.

Thus perished Turley, — a man worthy of a better fate.

Of the four other brave defenders of the mill, only two escaped, and they, too, almost by a miracle, later in the evening, and made their way northward.

"Well told, Karzy, but just a little too long," said Harold.

"So I was afraid," replied Karzy penitently. "Now, Mr. President, as a specimen of proper brevity, please give us one of your experience. Make it just as short as — it ought to be."

"The sarcasm is deserved, Karzy," said Harold good humoredly. "And it is all the sharper that I have been so indolent as to see but little worth telling. In fact, the most interesting thing I have seen since starting on this trip was in a lady's parlor up in Kansas."

"In a lady's parlor!" exclaimed Moses. "That sounds romantic. But I fear it is only a repetition of some of those experiences which brother Harold had while on our bycicle tour down East."

"No, brother Moses, quite another thing, I assure you. Listen, please. It is of interest as being one of the beginnings of a great future industry. As I came through Kansas, I left the railway at Lawrence and took a buggy ride down into the country, to look up a cousin of mine who has located in that quarter. On my way I got lost and had to beg a dinner at a farm-house away out on one of those boundless expanses which they call a county. There was but a single lady — I mean one lady — at the house. She entertained me very kindly, however, and after dinner and some current conversation, asked me if I would not like to take a look into her parlor. I thought that was sort of funny, but of course I said 'yes' and 'delighted I'm sure.'

"She opened the door, and, expecting to see the usually monotonous stuffed furniture, the bric-à-brac, the cabinet organ, the stereopticon, the photograph album, and the autograph album, for which I was already inwardly conning an appropriate sentiment from Tennyson, I looked in.

"Now if there is one thing more than another in which American ladies show an utter lack of originality it is in their parlors. All are after one model. If ever anywhere you find one differing from the standard, it is from the shape of the house or some other circumstance over which the lady herself had no control, and which you are sure to find her lamenting from a full heart.

"Judge of my surprise, then, to see three long tables covered with fresh green leaves, which somehow seemed all in motion! Even the window seats and the chairs were laden with green leaves and sprays, and as to the floor, it was covered with bare twigs. To my look of abject astonishment the lady laughed merrily. 'How do you like my furniture?' she said.

PUEBLO RESTORED.

"Something still more odd — for a parlor — had arrested my attention. It was a great green worm, somewhat like a maple-worm. It lay among the green leaves and was feeding on them. There were scores, hundreds, thousands of these great worms!

"'What are these, madam?' I asked.

"'My silkworms,' she said.

"'And this foliage?'

"'Mulberry leaves from these hedges round my garden. I bring in bushels of them every day. See the bare stems on the floor!'

"I began to comprehend.

"'Yes,' continued the lady, 'I started two years ago. George — that's my husband — laughed at me at first. He works hard; but unless it is a better year than last, I shall clear more off my cocoons than he will off his farm corn. I get seventy cents a pound for the cocoons. What's the good of a parlor shut up from one week's end to another!' she exclaimed. 'I have little time to sit in one. So I've *decorated mine with mulberry leaves!* and I have my attic and spare chamber all full of worms too. It is really pretty work to feed them.'

"'Well, this is, indeed, a new departure,' I said, — 'an original idea?'

"'No, I got it from the Mennonites, those Russian refugees who came to Kansas eight or ten years ago. They brought silk culture here, and imported the mulberry shrubs from Southern Russia. Their women reel the silk off the cocoon, but that takes a great deal of skill and practice. I prefer to sell my cocoons to the factory folks.'

"Surely, I thought, here is a hint for many a lady with a meagre family purse and a shut-up parlor. For the business requires little or no capital for starting."

"And now, Mr. Burleigh, what adventures have you met with of late?"

"No adventures," said Wash. "I met an old schoolmate, however, at Las Vegas."

"Well, that was pleasant, no doubt."

"Yes, it does seem good to meet an old chum. John Coombs and I were at the same school, as boys, and were at one time room-mates. I ran plump against him at the Plaza Hotel, but had not seen him for six years. He is located in Texas. 'I'm working a mine over there,' he said. 'A mine!' I replied. 'Gold or silver?'

"'Neither.'

"'What,—copper?' I asked.

"'No.'

"'Oh, coal, then.'

"'Wrong again; and it is n't iron, nor quicksilver, nor tin, nor plumbago,' said he.

"'Some metaphorical mine, I suppose; some bonanza in stocks, some horse ranch, some ostrich farm,' I said.

"'No, no; a real *bona-fide* mine. I'm getting out five tons of *ore* every day. Good ore, too; runs fifty dollars to the ton.'

"Of course I grew curious, hearing that. A fellow cannot travel here in New Mexico and Colorado without getting a touch of the mining fever. You know how it is yourself. This mining malaria is in the air out here. But not another word about his mine could I get out of John. 'Come over to see me,' said he. 'It's worth your while, really.' That was all he would say; he was only there for a few hours.

"I kept thinking about it all that evening; and next morning I looked up the trains and found that I could get round in three days. So I sent John a telegram and set off into Texas; there's where I've been.

"At D—— (the station where John had told me to get off if I came) I found him waiting for me with a wagon and two mules, and a ride of ten or twelve miles across the rolling prairie up into the *Llano estacado* brought us to his place. It was dark by the time

MINING IN THE SOUTHWEST.

we arrived; but I saw what looked to be a derrick and windlass for hoisting ore out of a shaft, also two or three sheds full of barrels and boxes.

"John was keeping bachelor's hall, with a Chinaman to cook for him, in a small board cottage near by. We had a very nice dinner and talked of old times at school till nine or ten o'clock. By that time, feeling pretty sleepy, I was ready to turn in. As yet John had said nothing of his mine. I concluded that he was keeping it all till the next day. My bunk was a comfortable one; and I slept soundly till about five o'clock the next morning, when I was awakened by a singular roaring noise. At first I thought that it was the wind — that a 'norther' had swept down upon us. But it sounded too steady for the wind. I lay and listened to it for some moments.

"John was up, moving about at the further end of the room. At length I called to him. 'Whatever is that noise?' I said. 'Is the chimney afire?'

"'Oh, no,' said he. 'That's my mine. It is *sucking in* now. At night from five to seven it *blows* off. From daybreak till after sunrise it *sucks in.*'

"'You must have a queer kind of engine,' I remarked.

"'Oh, it's not the engine at all. It's THE MINE.'

"'Look here, John, haven't you given me taffy enough about this mine?' I observed.

"'No taffy at all,' protested my friend. 'Come out and see it *suck in.*'

"I hastily dressed and followed him forth. The moment we opened the door and stepped out, the roaring noise was increased tenfold. It was still dark. The stars shone; the morning star had risen golden bright; while over the post oaks, off to the west, a segment of pale old moon hung like a whitish feather. But that noise! the whole air seemed to whirr to it, — to flutter deafeningly as when a train stops and the engine is very hot after a long run; you know what a strange detonating sort of noise the steam will make. This made me think of it. And all out to the left of the windlass frame there seemed to be a dense black cloud, which I took to be smoke, rising to the very zenith!

"John led the way out past the shed, for a hundred metres or more, till we came to the edge of a chasm, or *cañon*, in the limestone strata, several hundred feet wide and of unknown depth. Down into this chasm, at our very feet, the vast, black cloud, roaring, whizzing, was descending — not rising — rushing downward like water into the vortex of a tunnel, with a maelstrom-like force and velocity which was absolutely terrific! It gave me the same feeling, the same sense of power, as when years ago I first stood at

BATS GOING OUT.

the foot of Niagara and looked up at the plunging torrents of green water.

"'For heaven's sake, John, what is this thing?' I shouted.

"'Why, *bats!—bats!* Don't you see them! All down under here is a bat-cave — acres and acres of it. This cave is my mine. It's *sucking in,* now. The bats are going to roost. It's the guano, bat-guano, that I'm getting out. The floor of the cave is bedded with it. In some places it is ten feet deep, solid guano, and there's acres and acres of it. I've never half explored the cave yet.'

"'And these are all bats!' I exclaimed.

"'All bats. There are millions of them. They go out of the cave at nightfall in just such a stream, to catch flies, gnats, mosquitoes, what not in the way of insects, worms, and grubs, and come back at daybreak, as you see. Always just so, except in case of a heavy storm, and two or three weeks of the coldest winter weather, when they seem to hibernate and hang dormant from the roof of the cave.'

"It had grown a little lighter, and I saw now that the roaring, whirring cloud was indeed composed of bats. Above the noise of their wings I could now distinguish a multitudinous, mournful squeaking. There were thousands, yes, millions of them; and the velocity with which they shot down into the chasm from high up in the sky was absolutely appalling.

"How they managed to turn at the bottom of the chasm and dart laterally into the mouth of their cavern, I cannot understand. To look up into the cloud was like looking up into a dense, driving snowstorm. Overhead the air was full of them; and they came down each with a sharp *zerp-zerp!* It was wonderful, gentlemen, — about the most wonderful thing I ever witnessed. And that torrent of bats continued to whizz down like that for more than two hours steadily!

"It was only at sunrise that the cloud thinned off; and even then detached and scattered bands of them kept coming at intervals, till half past seven or eight o'clock.

"After breakfast we put on some old oilcloth suits, and taking each a lantern, went down by a circuitous path into the chasm, and came along to the mouth of the cave — a large, irregular orifice eight or ten feet in height, by thirty or forty in width, opening back into darkness, over great black bowlders. Numbers of bats were still flitting about; but it was not till we had scrambled into the cave fifty or sixty feet that we began to see them hanging in patches to the rocks overhead. The squealing was here incessant; and on thrusting up a lantern, hundreds of them would go flapping and scurrying along. Each bat hung to the roof by his claws, head downward. The further we went back into the cave, the denser grew the patches of bats, till at length the rocks above were seen to be covered with one continuous coat of them, often two or three thick; and in places they hung in festoons.

"Meantime the dropping of their *ordure* was incessant and sounded like rain. I saw, too, that the bottom of the cavern was alive with beetles and grubs, which seemed to be pulverizing the guano, which glistened in the light as if full of bits of mica. My friend said that this appearance was owing to the undigested wings of the insects upon which the bats feed. The entire place had a very strong odor of ammonia, with which the guano is powerfully impregnated — hence its value as a fertilizer. For it is for shipment as a fertilizer for worn-out soils that my friend is getting out the guano. At present there is a good market for it.

"Counting four hundred bats to the square yard — a low estimate — we reckoned that there were twenty millions of bats in those parts of the cave which we explored that day!

"No doubt that the bats have made this and scores of other similar caves which are known to exist in this section their habitat for ages. The great deposits of guano would seem to indicate as much.

"'Do they breed here?' I asked.

"For answer, John held up his lantern to a little cranny in the pitted, rough limestone roof; and I saw, back in a little hole, a most curious sight, — a female bat suckling four little pinkish-colored young, seemingly but a few days old. For as you know, the bat is a kind of winged mouse and brings forth its young as do mice.

"Every crack and hole is alive with just such pigmy families," my friend said.

I remained till night, and saw the innumerable troop depart on their nocturnal hunt after insects. Shortly after five o'clock they began to issue forth, in little squads at first, but soon with the same torrent-like rush with which I had beheld them come in at dawn; with this difference, however, in the morning they had seemed to return from a great height and to drop, or rather shoot down, to the mouth of their cave. But at eventide they rise out of the chasm and move off in a solid column close to the surface of the prairie. As far as I could see, they kept in this dense array; and my friend tells me that on several occasions when out in the country he has met this dusky column, moving swiftly on, yet still keeping together, at a distance of seven or eight miles from the cave.

How many billions of flies, gnats, and mosquitoes they snap up during a night I may safely leave to your conjecture, gentlemen. To me it was one of the most striking and interesting phases of animal life which I have ever witnessed; and I hope some naturalist will ere long make the habits of one of these innumerable bat-swarms a matter of careful study.

"Oddly enough," said Mr. Garland, "I have heard a bat story, with which there was connceted an Indian adventure. A young man, named Gillespie, up at Raton, told it. As to the bats, I thought the story an exaggeration at first; but after what Mr. Burleigh has himself seen, I see no reason to doubt it. This man, Gillespie, said that not very long after his parents moved into Texas (they came from New Jersey in 1872, I think he stated) he and his brother had a very narrow escape from some Indians. But I will try, if I can, to give the story in his words: —

My folks (he said) had located in the northern part of Kinney County, very near, if not over, the line in "the Bexar territory," as it is called, on a branch of the Nueces River. Further south the branch is dry toward the latter part of summer for miles and miles; but there are springs of good sweet water up here, which have not failed as yet.

My father had prospected these springs while out with a land-locating party the previous year; and, liking the place pretty well, he drove up a hundred and thirty head of cattle that fall, built a house during the winter, and moved in the following spring.

There is a good growth of mesquite, post-oak, and a few walnut trees about the spring heads. Our first house was built of mesquite logs, and the cattle-pens were set with mesquite and oak posts.

The timber is all in the valley, or *cañon*, as it is called, of the branch; the valley, or bottom, varying from half a mile to a mile in width. Bluffs, and, in some places, cliffs, a hundred feet and more, wall in the bottom on both sides. Back of the bluffs is the high plains land.

Through the spring and early part of summer the cattle are pastured up here, where the feed is then fresh. But later in the season, when the droughts set in, and through the winter, we depend on the bottom down in the *cañon*, along the branch, for feed and shelter for the stock from the northers.

One afternoon, near the last of June, — we had moved here in April, — my younger brother, Morris, thirteen years old, and I set off up the branch, taking each a tin bucket to gather cherries and "drool plums." The plums are nearly as large as pomegranates, and when they grow in fertile spots are quite well-flavored.

From two or three miles up the branch there is a considerable stretch along the bottom where fires had run ten or twelve years before. Wild-cherry, briars, and plums had now got in here; some of the finest wild cherries I have ever seen, almost as large as cultivated cherries, in fact, very dark red, and not at all bitter or puckery.

The *cañon* up there was narrower than down where the springs were; and from where we were getting the cherries it was not more than ten or fifteen rods to the foot of the crumbling sandstone crags which on that side enclosed the little interval.

Flocks of pigeons, and sometimes wild turkeys, came into the bottom at this time of year, and I had brought a shot-gun belonging to my Uncle Sidney. I could not find the cap-box, and so had only the charge in the gun, which was but a small single-barrelled piece.

We had gathered one bucket full of the drool plums, and had the other nearly filled with cherries, when we were not a little astonished at hearing the plaintive "blart" of a calf a little way off up the *cañon*; at least, it sounded exactly like that, yet all the cattle, as we supposed, were four or five miles below and on the prairie.

GOING TO THE TABLE LANDS.

A SURPRISE.

"It's one of our little bossies strayed away from the old cow!" exclaimed Mot; and upon that we left our cherries and started to find the calf.

We went some little distance calling, "Boss! boss! co-boss!" But the bush clumps and great clusters of dagger-grass were so thick there that it was difficult to see ahead much. At length Mot went out close to the crags, while I kept along by the branch through tall raspberry briars.

We had not been separated long, however, when I heard the same plaintive "baa-a-a-a!" again, out near where Mot was, as I thought. Upon this I turned to go to him, but had hardly taken ten steps when I heard him give a loud screech! Then another and another, as if frantic with fright. I cocked my shot-gun and ran to help him, for I thought most likely he was frightened by a "rattler."

In a moment he came plump against me round a great bunch of cactuses, running swiftly and pale as death. Before he could speak an old Indian in a calico shirt, with a long rope halter in his hand, came in sight in full chase after him.

That was the kind of calf we had heard blart!

The shot-gun was all cocked, and without a second's thought I fired at the Indian. The turkey-shot, no doubt, hit him, for he stopped short and dropped his rope.

Just then another Indian, a young fellow, not full grown, came in sight from behind a clump of bushes. He had a gun. Other redskins set up a yell not far off when they heard me fire.

The instant I had fired I turned and ran after Mot, and threw the shot-gun into some briar bushes.

We struck into an old cattle-path, through the thickets along the foot of the crags, and ran for dear life for eighty or a hundred rods, when, to our dismay, we heard the Indians racing past us through the cherry trees off a few rods to our right. They had outrun and gone past us.

With this we turned and ran back the other way, dreadfully scared and out of breath, and coming presently to a dark hole under the overhanging rocks clambered into it — to hide.

In our flurry and fright we did not at first think of our tracks along the moist ground at the foot of the crags. Then it came into my mind that the Indians would see them and certainly find us; and I did not dare to leave our hiding-place for fear they might already have returned in search of us.

The hole into which we had crept was six or eight feet broad, but so low we had been obliged to bend to enter it. On first getting in amongst the damp, mossy rocks, we could not see anything it was so dark; but after being in there a few minutes, I began dimly to discern that the aperture led back further, over and among other rocks. So we clambered back — as our eyes became accustomed to the gloom, forty or fifty feet, where the air was very chilly and damp. We could stand up here, and as we groped back still further, came where we could not touch the rocks overhead.

We were in a cave. Our feet on the rocks raised strange echoes; even our whisperings were mysteriously repeated about us. I thought, too, that I heard a curious hissing and faint squeaks like mice.

"O-o-gh, — something soft flapped in my face!" Mot cried out; but ere we had time to think much of these things we heard the Indians outside. First a whoop which had a strange, far-off sound, then a darkening of the light at the mouth of the cave, and a scraping noise on the outer rocks, as if some of them were crawling in.

They had found our hiding-place.

For some minutes we heard them talking. Then the hole darkened again. There was another scraping noise, and soon one of the savages came in sight, crawling over the great bowlders in the low opening of the cavern, with his gun in his hand.

I felt sure he could not see us; but we moved slowly away and groped along for a number of yards. Coming to where there were some loose stones under foot, I took a good large one in each hand and stood still.

The Indian came crawling in, reaching up his hands this side and that, till he came where the passage was broader and higher. Here he stood upright, and thrusting out his gun to feel his way, came forward, step by step.

I stood still till he had come within thirty feet of me, and then I threw at him with all my might one of my big stones.

It hit him full in the chest, fairly knocking him off his feet on the slippery rocks. His gun flew out of his hand, and went clattering on the bowlders; and the way that redskin scrabbled up and went out over the rocks, and along that hole, was far from slow, I promise you! I let my other stone fly after him. When he had got nearly out, he gave a yell, and the others outside yelled.

We did not see or hear anything more of them for some minutes, and hoped they had concluded not to attempt to enter the cave again; but they were not so easily thrown off. Before a long time had passed we saw one of them crawling into the mouth of the cave, with a torch in one hand and a gun in the other. Behind him came another redskin.

Mot crept in back of the great bowlder against which we stood, and I got more stones to throw; but with their torches the Indians would soon have hunted us out, had it not been for a most singular thing which suddenly occurred.

TROPICAL SCENERY.

No sooner were the two Indians fairly in the cave with their torches than there came a rumble like low thunder; then such a prodigious squeaking and hissing that, along with a whirring noise, we were quite deafened by it.

In an instant the whole cavern was full of fluttering wings, which flapped in our faces and fairly took away our breath. I fought with both hands for a moment or two, then curled down beside a rock. Once or twice above the sharp squeaking and rumbling I thought I heard the Indians yell. Their torches were put out, and I could not see them. How they got out I'm sure I don't know; for I do not think I could have stood up and kept my feet. There was a perfect tornado of bats.

And for nearly two hours that same stunning, fluttering, and strange squeaking noise continued without a moment's cessation. We lay as close as we could to the rocks, to keep out of the way of the excited creatures.

It was a bat-cave, similar to those since discovered in Uvalde and Bandera Counties. Probably it was the torches which startled the bats. I have no doubt there were a million bats in that cave. It is their home by day.

After long time — hours, it seemed to us — the place cleared of them somewhat, and the awful rumble gradually ceased. As evening approached the innumerable army had gone forth for the night.

My brother and I crept out near the mouth of the cave. It was dark; yet we did not dare to venture forth, for we were afraid the Indians might still be near. Bats, in little flights, went fluttering out past us — belated stragglers which had overslept.

At length I heard father and Uncle Sidney shouting for us at a distance; and after looking cautiously out of the cave and listening for some minutes, we ventured to crawl forth and run to them.

They had not seen the Indians, but had found our cherry-pails.

Next day we recovered the shot-gun, and Uncle Sidney found the Indian's rifle in the cave. It had a solid silver clamp on the breech worth nearly fifteen dollars.

The bats, no doubt, saved us our scalps that time. Often since I have been near the cave at sunset, to watch "the squeakers" come out of it. A gun fired into the mouth of the cavern will, at that time of day, cause them to come out. One has abundant need to get out of the way when they start. A stream of them, the full size of the hole, packed close together, will pour out for two hours steadily. There seems no end of them.

For anything we know the cave extends a great distance under-ground. The bats roost there, clinging to its sides and roof.

"New Mexico and this West Texas country is indeed a remarkable land," said Brett. "Those are wonderful facts about the bats; but as it happens I can match your bat story with a *bee* story, which, however, ends in a bear story. But never mind that part. I think I can safely vouch for the truth of my account; for I was sure I saw strict veracity gleaming in the eye of my informant, whose name, by the way, is Cantwell. But rest assured there is no *cant* to his narrative."

Four of us (he said) — my ranch partner, Alfred Dinsmore, and myself, with a young German house-carpenter, named Wert Auspach, and a colored boy, called "Grant," — had set out that day for a load of honey.

A *load* of honey will sound oddly, perhaps; but that is the way we get it here. Wild honey, rich stores of it, is laid up by the native bees. The settlers often have resort to a "bee-tree" when their stock of sugar and molasses runs low. The honey is drained from the comb and put away in jars, and the wax makes excellent candles.

Twelve or thirteen miles up north of our location, in the *cañon* of Lipan Creek (headquarters of Wichita River), there is a "bee's nest" which has supplied us and the families of three other stockmen for the last four years.

This enormous bee-hive is in the cliff, on the north side of the *cañon*, fronting south. The entrance to it is up some forty feet above the creek-bed, where there is a horizontal crack eight or ten inches wide, running along the face of the precipice for four or five hundred feet. This crack opens back into recesses in the shattered crags behind; and here the bees, colony on colony, have their nests and have laid up honey for many years.

By going round and operating from the top of the cliff we have at odd times dislodged considerable portions of the rock with blasts of gunpowder and crowbars — sufficient to secure many hogsheads of comb.

Still deeper down in great pits and holes there seems to be a vast deposit of old, thick, black candied honey, which has been drained from the tiers of comb above year after year.

Lower down the face of the cliff the honey, especially on very hot days, weeps and oozes out at little cracks and seams of the fissured sandstone — so much so that the creek-bank is there completely honey-soaked, and the water for a mile or two below will at times be perceptibly sweetened. Much of this escaping honey the bees themselves carry back up the face of the cliff.

On a pleasant June day the *cañon*, and high above it, the air will be darkened by the in-coming and out-going clouds of bees, millions on millions of them,

SCENES IN NEW MEXICO.

along the whole length of the crevice. The ordinary drowsy hum of a hive is here intensified to a deep, solemn roar, distinctly audible for a mile below.

To go honey-gathering there on a summer's day might be a perilous business. We have always made our raids on the nest during the cold weather, generally on some chilly day toward Christmas, when the bees are lying torpid and a winter silence has fallen upon this whole vast apiary.

It was one of the last days of November; and when we started that morning the weather was quite warm, almost "muggy," with a thin bluish fog rising from the prairie, which had lately been burned over and lay coal-black under foot.

But we had not gone more than eight or ten miles when a "norther" came down on us in full blast. The first we saw of it was a sudden whirling of the fog over the tops of the mesquites out to our left. Then came a puff of cold air, as damp and chilling as when in summer one steps into a cellar.

A minute later this premonitory whiff was followed by a second puff, a perfect gust, which sent our hats whirling, and upset the half-hogshead off the spring-board.

The norther was upon us!

That is the way these freezing gales always come here; sometimes they don't even give one time to get on a great coat and mittens. How cold they are, and how they cut through a body! In half an hour the mercury will fall forty and fifty degrees.

Often rain, sleet, and sometimes snow come with it.

No one tries to do anything during a norther here. You cannot even get a blacksmith to shoe your horse while a norther is blowing, and it often blows three days at a bout.

The folks "den up" and keep a great fire going. You will not see a person stirring out anywhere, — no old settler at least, in the village.

When the norther struck us, we set out to go back home; but as the *cañon* was now no great distance ahead, we drove on and got into that at a place about two miles below the great "bee's nest."

The cliffs here broke the force of the gale, and selecting a place where a big rick of drift stuff had been lodged against the rocks by floods, we built a roaring fire and made a shed, partly of the half-hogsheads and spring-boards, and partly of drift-wood and brush. Here we made ourselves comfortable, gave the mules their corn, and had no thoughts of going up on the prairie for honey or anything else while the gale held.

The crag on the side against which we had our fire was sixty or seventy feet high, but, as I have mentioned above, was here all along much fissured and cracked, showing crevices and crannies where the broken strata had worked apart, often three and four feet in width. The drift-rick, which served us for wood-pile, burned well, — the blaze mounting half way up the cliff, and casting a warm glow back into our shed.

Here, throughout the rest of the day and evening, while the gusts howled across the *cañon* from out over the prairie to north'ard, we lay at our ease and told stories, going sound asleep at last, wrapped up in our buffalo skins.

Some hours must have passed ; for our big fire had burned down low, when I was roused by a scratching, raking noise on the rocks in front of our shed. Before I was as yet half awake something — it was so dark I could not tell what, but some heavy animal, I felt sure — came down the rocks and fell partly into the open front of our shed, and right on Auspach's (the German) extended feet and ankles.

With that Wert jumped to get up and gave a shout, and we all arose, fumbling for our guns. But before Anse or I or any of us had gained our legs, down came the shed, the half-hogsheads we had brought for our honey, our tilted-up spring-board wagon, brush, and all.

Who had the most to do with knocking it down I am sure I don't know. It was a free scrabble. One of the half-hogsheads tipped over in such a way as to completely shut Grant, the colored boy, under it all but his shanks ; and as the fore-wheels of the spring-board lay partly across the bottom of the hogshead, he was caught fast.

The noise he made was as nothing compared with the racket the German was making ; for the other half-hogshead had partly fallen over him, and he was kicking at an unknown wild beast whose growls mixed with his shouts.

"Arnse, vere bees you ?" we heard him calling out in reproachful tones.

The moment we had extricated ourselves from the brush and stakes, Dinsmore and I sprang to our feet and tried to take in the situation.

It was too dark to see much. The brush was snapping and the half-hogshead bobbing up and down ; and just then the savage, growling head of some animal was thrust repeatedly out betwixt the spokes of one of the hind wheels of the capsized spring-board.

Anse, who had seized upon the camp-axe, let it drive at the growler's head. His first stroke knocked two spokes out of the wheel. At its next plunge the animal came head and shoulders through the gap ; but I had secured one of the guns, and at this juncture, by good luck, shot it dead.

Almost with the report Wert, who had been making frantic efforts to get out through the brush on the back side, scrambled to his feet, shouting, —

A ROUGH ENCOUNTER.

"Sharles, pe careful vare you shoots! Whole dozen tem puckshots go puzz py my ear!"

"It's a bear," said Alf, peeping between the spokes of the wheel; but before we had time to haul out the carcass, or even get Grant from under the hogshead tub, another bear came sliding down the rocks with a scratch and a growl, and fell sprawling into the ashes and still glowing embers of the fire. A perfect smother of ashes and coals flew up. It must have been a warm lighting for the old chap's feet.

He whirled round with a low yelp, and leaped out over some logs at the lower end of our shed. I just had time to cock my left barrel and fire as his hind legs disappeared down over the logs. We heard him give a growl when the shot

"SHARLES, PE CAREFUL VARE YOU SHOOTS!"

struck him, but had no time to look for him or even see where he went to, for Wert had set up a great outcry.

"Queek, Arnse! queek, Sharles, mit yours goon! In der holler up ze rock! Dou you hears him yow? Anoder one's coming down!"

Surely enough, there was another looking out of a great fissure, up twenty-five or thirty feet, growling and making as if to descend. I could plainly see its head, and a moment after it turned to come down tail-first.

"Zhoust you hark, poys!" exclaimed Wert. "Only hear dem *sing!*"

If there had been a whole menagerie shut up back amongst those rocks it could hardly have made more *music*,— growling, whining, roaring, and *yowling!*

"There's an awful big den in there! and it's biling over full of 'em!"

Every minute or two a head would pop out in sight from the crevice. The firing and the noise had stirred them up. It looked as if the animals had climbed up to this den over the heap of driftwood which our fire had burned up. The smoke and fire flaming up to the mouth of the hole had kept them in during the first part of the night; or else they had all been comfortably asleep in there, passing the norther. But now they evidently all wanted to come out — hungry, perhaps.

During the forenoon we got logs and stuff from the drift-ricks lower down, which we set up in such a way that we could climb to the entrance of the den. All being quiet there now, Alf climbed up — to reconnoitre the brutes.

There was a pretty large fissure which opened back between and over great detached masses of rock for eighteen or twenty feet. In back of these, lower down, there seemed to be a big, black hole, evidently a considerable cavern.

I now climbed up, and together we peeped and peeked about for some time. When we looked down into the dark hole there would be low growling.

Three or four hours were spent. We found that it was no use trying to shoot them in the dark. There was a cave back in there as large as a hall — a great irregular cavity, emitting a very strong *bearish* stench.

In the afternoon we assailed them on a new tack. Wert and Grant split up a lot of wood which, with their assistance, we carried up our log ladder, half a cord of it at least, and then pitched it into the cavern. A brand was then fetched up, and we soon had a bonfire going which lighted up the whole inside of the den. From where we stood up in the fissure the bears could now be seen crouching behind the black bowlders and in the far corners of the cave, snarling uneasily at the fire. I counted five, and Alf soon made out two more.

To shoot game thus cornered up may be deemed an unsportsmanlike method of hunting; but my friend and myself were troubled by no such scruples.

An hour later we hauled *seven* bears — dead ones — out of that cave, which, added to those already secured, made *ten* carcasses.

They were, with but one exception, remarkably fat bears, too. Their flesh had a noticeably *sweet* taste, which we attributed to their getting so much honey hereabouts.

CHAPTER II.

EL PASO. — "BROKE UP ON TIME." — A "SOLIMETER." — MEXICAN CUSTOM-HOUSE CHARGES. — APACHE ATROCITIES. — IN A DESERT. — AN IMMENSE STOCK FARM. — MEXICAN POST-OFFICES. — CHIHUAHUA. — THE HOTEL. — A MOONLIGHT PROMENADE. — AN AWKWARD RENCONTRE. — TWO ROUTES INTO MEXICO. — A DISCUSSION. — DIVISION OF THE PARTY. — OFF FOR THE CITY OF MEXICO BY DILIGENCE.

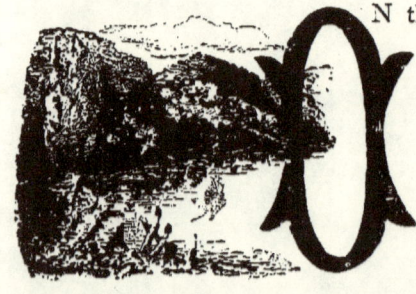

ON the morning of the 26th we bade adieu to our comfortable quarters in the *Las Cruces*, which had come to seem quite like home to us, and, getting into a 'bus, were driven from the Santa Fé depot across the ford of the Rio Grande to the pretty new station of the recently finished line of El Ferrocarril Central Mexicano, which at the date of our visit had begun running its trains from El Paso down to Chihuahua, the capital of the Mexican State of the same name, a distance of two hundred and twenty-five miles south.

By mistake we did not get off till near train time, and the Mexican custom-house officer on the south bank of the river delayed us still further while he inspected our travelling-bags. Then we had the narrow streets of the Mexican town of El Paso to wind through.

"Driver, what time is it now?" Moses called out.

The driver, a typical New Mexican, shook his head gloomily. "We're all broke up on time here," he said. "All broke up. What kind of time do you want, sir?"

"What kind have you got?"

"All kinds. Thar's local time. That varies somewhat, 'cording to gents' watches, you know, but I calls it (looking) 7.50 A.M. But the Santa Fé folks here run their trains on Jefferson City time. It ought to be 8.48 by them, I expect. But perhaps as yer goin' by the *Central* you wants their time. That's City o' Mexico time, 'bout 8.20, say. But lots o' gents wants Chicago time an' keeps ter that. By that 'tis now 'bout 8.54, mebbe. But ask most any of these western-through gents on the Southern Pacific and they'd say 6.50 A.M.; for they haint changed their watches, an' gives you San Francisco time. 'Though 'bout's many more mought say 9.50 for they're just in from the East and have New York time. We figgers it as snug's we can on 'em an' trys ter fit 'em out. But gents gets left every day on it, an' there's no end o' swarin'. We're all broke up. I dunno what we'll do on it yet — onless the buys goes an' gets watches that keeps all the kinds o' time ter wunst. For let a gent get a little flurried an' he's dead sure to go an' add the diffrunce o' time on the wrong end.

"But mornin's at the hotel is when we has the wust rows, callin' gents for the trains. They leaves word at the office ter be called at five, or half-past, or mebbe six. We goes ter knockin' fur 'em as near's we can figger it, fur their trains. But like's any way they all comes down madder'n hens. Some's an hour too airly an' some's got left an' has ter lay round all day cussin about it. I dunno what we'll do. Thar's no gauge yet."

"What you want here, driver," said Stein, "is a *solimeter*."

"I expect so," said the man, confidently. "Ken ye give us the name of the kempany that makes 'em?"

"I am sorry to say I cannot," said Stein, "for the reason that they are not yet made. It remains for some enterprising American to make them — and make his fortune at the same time. What we need is a watch that — something as a compass always points to the pole — shall always indicate solar time according to the position of the sun in the sky, or rather according to the relative position of the sun and any given place on the earth. Noon with such a watch would always be when the sun had reached its highest point in the heavens; and midnight when it stood at the opposite point beneath the earth. No matter how far such a watch was carried, east or west, it would always indicate correct local time by the sun. Once such watches were universally adopted, the whole problem of varying time would be solved."

The driver gazed suspiciously at Stein, but seeing no wild rolling of his eyes began to lash the horses.

Moses laughed. "You've unsettled his peace of mind," said he.

"But that really is an idea, Stein," Brett remarked. "If it were n't quite so universally big I think something might be done with it. What did you call it, — that new ideal watch, I mean?"

"Oh, I called it a *solimeter* — sun measurer," said Stein, laughing. "I expect to be carrying one some twenty years hence."

Meantime we were going on at a great pace, but soon pulled up.

"Central Mexican station, gents," the driver shouted. "Just in time to slip aboard. Fifty cents all round, please."

Some of our shrewd Americans who — now that Mexico is being opened up by railroads — are planning to ship in goods and sell them at a handsome profit, may be taken aback when they come to pay duties at the frontier. Mexican duties are enormous. On many articles they are as high as one hundred per cent of the value of the goods; and the Mexican officials *rate the value to suit themselves.*

We saw an example of this at the station that morning. An enterprising fellow-countrywoman of our own, hailing from Chicago, but a very decent sort of person, nevertheless, and very comely, too, was on her way to Chihuahua to open an American boarding-house. Among other articles she had three stoves, not very large ones; and those Mexican officers charged her seventy-five dollars *duties* on those three stoves!

EL PASO.

The poor woman first turned red, then pale; but there was no appeal. It was pay or lose them. The sympathies of our fellow-clubsman, Moses, were so strongly aroused at the sight of the woman's evidently genuine, though quiet distress, that we, his friends, had no small task to get him into the car and prevent another war with Mexico there on the platform of the station.

"'Tis the most barefaced, villanous transaction which I ever saw perpetrated under the sanction of law! Such a government deserves to be *smashed*, and I would like to assist!" raved Moses.

We had to distract his attention by telling him of an Indian outrage which had occurred that morning up near Rincon, which we had passed on our way down. The Apaches had burned a house and killed a woman and two children. These were renegade Apaches that had run away from the reservation. It was a satisfaction to know that the wretches would soon be hunted down and shot. For General Crook now has nearly all the Apaches on their reservation; and all the "bucks" are compelled to wear a numbered tag, which they have to show up conspicuously twice a day; otherwise, there is an Indian hunt directly. Of all ruthless, bloodthirsty beasts which have thus far inhabited the earth, including tigers, jaguars, and grizzly bears, none have ever yet been worthy to be named with an Apache when he smells the blood of a white family.

Upon the same morning, too, we heard that a party of them had killed forty-six persons, not far out of Chihuahua. The Apaches not only ravage Arizona and New Mexico, but Old Mexico as well, for a distance of four hundred miles south of the frontier. The Mexican government does not mince matters, but keeps a standing reward up for Apache heads. Very few are brought in, however; for the government is loth to send the soldiers out after Indians lest the rascals should desert across the frontier, the average *soldado Mexicano* being much inclined to take French leave of his country's service. Upon quitting the station the train soon steams out into the desert,

78   THE KNOCKABOUT CLUB IN THE TROPICS.

for by that word the country for the first eighty miles south of El Paso is best described. Scattered bunches of soap-weed and here and there a cactus, or a thorn bush, are the only vegetation. Sand hills, shifting in the wind are seen at intervals; but for the most part

A DESERT.

the country is a dreary, waterless plain, bounded around by jagged purple-hued peaks, which give the landscape a singularly wild and barren aspect. One's first impressions of Mexico, entered from this point, are dreary. Artesian wells might perhaps redeem this arid tract. Stein, indeed, thought he saw a chance for a fortune by purchasing this desert — for a trifle — and boring wells which would (or ought to, according to his theory) give a copious supply of water for irrigation.

"You forget the duties!" interrupted Moses. "These Mexicans would charge you so much for duties on your pump-augurs that they would burst your whole business."

Moses is a free-trader — since coming to Mexico.

But though a desert, the country is a fine one for building a railroad in; and it would look as if the Nickerson combination, with a promised subsidy of $15,200 to the mile from the Mexican government, had a good thing on their railroad.

"A good thing if they get the money," said Moses. "But I respectfully submit that twenty million dollars is a good deal to get of such a country and such a government. In ninety-nine years, too, the line reverts to the Mexican government — if there be one in existence by that time."

"It is said that thus far the Mexicans have acted in perfect good faith and very honorably toward the American company," Harold remarked. "I see no reason to suppose that they will not fulfil their pledges."

Between El Paso and Chihuahua there are but few way-stations, — only one, in fact, that can fairly be called such. There are water-tanks and sidings after every fifteen or twenty miles; and at one of these two freight cars have been converted into a "dining-room" for travellers. But, for the most part, the train appears to make one straight run, without change of locomotive, for Chihuahua.

After the first seventy-five or eighty miles the line enters the great estate of the present governor of the State of Chihuahua. The land begins to lose somewhat of its desert aspect, and shows scanty grass. The mountains too are rugged, bare, and sombre; and here and there herds of cattle are seen. These latter grow more and more numerous, till at length the locomotive is compelled to keep up a continuous piping of its whistle to frighten the animals off the line.

There are said to be thirty thousand head of cattle and two hundred thousand sheep on this one estate, which is of fully ten thousand square miles' extent. Not even our most ambitious fellow-citizens dare dream of a farm like that! The people on it are all "peons" (laborers and herdsmen), and are about as much a part of the estate as the cattle, — more so, even, for they vote as the governor wishes; and he does not have to go round among them with his hat in his hand and promise them all postmasterships. For one reason, there are no post-offices. Only two mails a week leave Chihuahua City itself, — the capital of the State, and a town of twenty thousand inhabitants!

The post-office there is refreshingly primitive. Go in and ask for a letter, and the postmaster hands you the entire mail and lets you *see for yourself.* You take what belongs to you — if you are honest — or carry off the whole outfit if otherwise. The postmaster does not even do you the politeness to watch you, but sits at his ease acting as if the mail were a burden he would gladly be rid of. Nobody steals letters, however, — for the reason, maybe, that everybody knows better than to send money or anything else of any value in a Mexican mail.

The run from El Paso to Chihuahua was made in ten hours. It was seven o'clock and moonlight when we reached the station, which is a mile to the north of the town, across the river.

Seen by moonlight Chihuahua is a white town, and at a distance might be taken for a clean one, — for a large New England village, in fact. This resemblance vanishes utterly on a nearer approach, however; for the houses are all built either of stone or adobe, have flat roofs, and are plastered with lime on the outside, or else whitewashed. The windows too are secured by strong iron grates on the front, so that a street here has a decidedly jail-like air.

The principal edifices are the church, the *cabildo* (calaboose), with which is connected the town hall, alcalde's office, etc., the mint, the governor's house, and the structures used as hotels. These latter and the church front on the *plaza*, or public square, at the centre of the town. To one of the former, called the "American House," we were driven in a truly American 'bus ("fifty cents all round") from the station, and arrived just as the really very fine military band stationed at the plaza with the Mexican troops began to play for the evening, according to usual custom. The moonlight, the plaza with the green trees, fountains, and sauntering crowds of señores and señoritas, all in

CHIHUAHUA.

the humble presence of the massive double-towered old church, where the odd, silver-toned bells seemed constantly striking the hours and the quarters, made a very pleasing scene for a late November night.

The interior of the "American House" was not as pleasing. This and all houses here are built about a *patio*, or open court-yard. The rooms open out by folding-doors, defended by iron gratings upon a balcony surrounding this patio on the inside. Few of the apartments have windows; the doors have to suffice to admit light. The floors are of tiles. To say that the beds are as hard as a board is an injustice — to the board. The pillows are of sodden wool; and the rooms have a damp, never-been-aired smell, to which was superadded the languishing odor of Mexico.

"It isn't garlic, exactly," said Stein, "and it isn't mustiness. My nose doesn't quite make it out."

"It is the country," said Moses. "It is Mexico. I've smelled it ever since I crossed the line."

For supper they gave us a mixture of American and Mexican dishes; among the latter black beans (*frigoles*) prepared in a manner to impart a flavor which suggested the "odor of the country," abovementioned. Still, these were rather palatable.

The frigoles eaten, we went out to see the town and hear the music on the plaza. While promenading, the party became separated into twos and threes, and went different ways. But by ten o'clock all had got back to the hotel, except Moses, the "theolog," and Karzy. We went to bed thinking they would soon come in; but about midnight Stein, with whom Karzy was to share a room, came round and waked us all.

"Karzy hasn't come in yet," he said, "nor Moses, nor Mr. Garland. Something's wrong, I am afraid."

We all got up, feeling a good deal concerned. No one was stirring in the house, so we poked our way out into the street and across the plaza. Here we ran into a night watchman, or *sereno*, who would no doubt have arrested us had we not been quite so numerous. He was a formidable fellow, armed with a carbine, revolver, and I know not what other weapons, also a lantern, very like those made of tin and used in New England sixty years ago.

From the plaza we went out past the church and dived in and out through a maze of dirty, narrow streets, making a complete circuit of the town, in fact, and returning to the hotel, without seeing or hearing anything of the missing ones. Indeed, we might have anticipated the result of our search, had we coolly considered it.

To forcibly wake the landlord was our next effort — and it was an effort, indeed! As might have been anticipated again, we got no information from him. I doubt if we even succeeded in making him at all understand the case.

The balance of the night was spent in anxious conjecture and consultation, in the several rooms of the party; and with earliest peep of day we all sallied forth again to make a thorough canvass of the city, determined to find the absent members of the Club, alive or dead. Stein and the writer proceeded to the alcalde's office, and from the guard (the alcalde himself was not yet astir) we heard something which much alleviated our fears, — namely, that three young *Americanos* were in the calaboose!

"Let's go home to breakfast," said Stein, "and allow justice to take its course;" for we now felt rather vexed than alarmed.

While at breakfast the three lamented ones came in. That they looked a trifle cheap (*baratos*) rather did them credit, we thought. Apparently they had agreed among themselves not to give a full account of their adventures. But we knew so much already, and greeted them with such a roar of inquiry, that the "theolog." at once made a clean breast of everything, at the same time expressing his regrets in a very handsome manner for the anxiety they had caused us.

The gist of their story may be given in a few words: After separating from us the previous evening on the plaza, they had walked a little, and, wishing to see the sights, of course had stepped into a saloon, or whatever else it may be called, where a game of three-card monté was in progress. They went in, not to play, but simply to watch the Mexicans for a moment. The room was an inner one, with a rather devious entry-way; and they had been there but a minute or two when a Mexican officer (a brother of the governor of the State, as we learned), who was betting rather heavily, became enraged with the "dealer," charging him with cheating at the cards. There was a moment's altercation, when the officer drew a revolver and shot the dealer three or four times, killing him. Other shots were fired. There was a general *mêlée*. Karzy says that Moses got under the table. Moses does not deny it; he remarked that he had no ambition to stop a bullet which was none of his business. It has been intimated, too, that Karzy was seen trying to get through the one window; but as that was amply provided with bars on the outside, he did not succeed in escaping that way. Before anybody could get out of the place a squad of *policia* ran in, and, holding the door, bagged the entire party, — *Mexicanos y Americanos, todos*, — and marched them all off to the calaboose together.

AN INTERIOR.

There they passed the night in a room with a stone floor, without beds or chairs, squatted against the wall. But immediately that the morning examination of the case was begun, the Americans were discharged and bidden to go about their business.

"We were served perfectly right," said Mr. Garland, in conclusion. "We had no business whatever in such a place. It ought to be a good lesson for us. I only regret the uneasiness we have caused the rest of the party."

No one could stand out against an apology so manfully made. We unanimously forgave them.

The day was spent looking about Chihuahua, though there was little more to see; and during the afternoon we held a council to determine the route of our journey to the City of Mexico. To proceed there directly by land would necessitate a journey of some eight hundred miles by *diligencia*, a kind of overland coach to Lagos, or Aguas Calientes, the most northern point then reached by the southern division of the new Mexican Central railroad. This journey would occupy eighteen or twenty days, and was sure to be very tiresome. The route, too, was said to be infested by Apaches and Mexican bandits, who often robbed the *diligencias*.

Brett, Harold, the Cadet, and Wash. were in favor of trying the overland route, and fighting the bandits, if necessary. They liked the idea of roughing it through the interior of Mexico.

The balance of the party, however, deemed it better — more comfortable and more interesting — to go back to El Paso, and thence journey by rail to New Orleans. From this place they could go by steamer, either to Vera Cruz direct, or, better still, go to Cuba for a few weeks, and thence to Vera Cruz. From Vera Cruz it would be an easy trip by rail up to the City of Mexico, through some of the grandest scenery in the world.

Both routes had their obvious advantages, and these were warmly urged on either hand.

"Of course there is a pleasure in journeying all together," Stein remarked at length. "But in this case I am inclined to think it will be best to divide the party, and let one branch take one route and the other the other route. More will be seen so, and when we meet in Mexico there will be more of interest to communicate mutually."

This suggestion was at first vigorously opposed by several of the party, but finally adopted as being the best plan under the circumstances.

GETTING A START.

The *diligencia* leaves Chihuahua at nine in the evening; and as it was already late, little time remained. We took dinner together; and there was a general inspection of carbines, revolvers, and other accessories of stage-coaching through a rough country, by our four comrades who had chosen the interior route; and then leave-taking.

The *diligencia* was at the plaza at eight o'clock. It took the people in charge of it an hour to hitch up the horses and mules, and get ready for a start. They first put two horses on the pole; then, after ten or fifteen minutes, they put three mules abreast ahead of the span. Finally, they hitched four more horses abreast, as leaders — nine in all. The *diligencia* itself differed not in appearance from a battered stage-coach in the United States.

Meanwhile our four comrades procured their tickets, and took their stations on top of the coach. "We will meet you in the City of Mexico," was the mutual promise on both sides.

At last the word to go was given, "*Hoopla! Hola! Hoorey!*" Whips cracked; the bystanders yelled; but the horses, or else the mules, balked; and the whole team got in a snarl. The driver shouted and lashed the beasts. The bystanders, too, fifty or sixty in number, took a hand and stoned the horses on both sides. The *diligencia* described a circle over the cobble-stones. At last they straightened out and went off like a shot, — "*hip, hola*," out of town into the moonlit night. And that was the last we saw of those fellows for many a day.

The remainder of the party, including the scribe, went back to El Paso, and thence to New Orleans in three days, by rail.

CHAPTER III.

CHRISTMAS-TIDE IN NEW ORLEANS. — HORNS AND POWDER-BURNING. — PASSPORTS FOR HAVANA. — OFF FOR CUBA. — THE EADS JETTIES. — CEDAR KEYS AND KEY WEST. — THE FLORIDA SHIP-CANAL.

TO a Northerner New Orleans seems to be the most un-American city in the country. Its quaintly-roofed and balconied houses, with their tall, green-roofed cisterns for rain-water; its orange gardens; its droll little milk-carts, and its cemeteries with their streets and squares of house-shaped marble tombs, placed high and dry above the black, water-soaked ground, — all these and a hundred other *outré* features combine to give the Crescent City a character of its own, and to declare the dissimilar ancestry of its people.

But the oddest feature, as perhaps some of our younger readers will think, is the manner in which the boys and girls of New Orleans celebrate Christmas; for with them Christmas is much like the Fourth of July in other parts of the country. They celebrate it with horns, rockets, torpedoes, and, in short, all the powder-burning with which the national birthday is commonly ushered in in the Northern States.

The custom of burning so much powder — the symbol of war and destruction — upon the day on which Christ was born strikes one, at first, as singularly *mal apropos*. But young America is not apt to stickle on points of poetic harmony; and after all, it is the spirit

NEW ORLEANS.

more than the mere *method* of a celebration which counts. The spirit (if it can in any way be estimated by the noise made) is certainly present in full power. This year (1882) Christmas Day and the two previous days were one continual explosion of fireworks, one constant conclamation of fish-horns, bugles, fifes, and every other wind instrument. Processions of a hundred, even three and four hundred boys and men, all provided with horns of all lengths and degrees of raucity, paraded the streets and squares, harping in loud, if not solemn, choir. The girls, too, and even the young ladies, were seen sporting gayly-ornamented horns. Men of fifty, with beards quite gray, joined in the general clangor. Dissonance with all its ear-splitting horrors reigned. Neither by day nor night did the fanfarade cease.

Terrific at first, one soon grew accustomed to it; and when once the spirit of the jollification had taken possession of one's mind, the hubbub attuned itself to something like harmony. For it was plain to see that the children enjoyed it immensely. New Orleans, too, it must be remembered, has from its dissimilar associations never entered much into the spirit of our Fourth of July celebrations; and doubtless the young people of every city must have at least one day to blow horns and make a noise.

On going to take tickets for Havana by the steamer *Morgan* we were told that it would be impossible to proceed thither without *passports*. The Spanish authorities in Cuba rigidly insist that all foreigners, Americans in particular, shall present documents from their government certifying to their names and general good character. In Mexico, on the contrary, no passports are required. The system may be a good one; but the motive on the part of the Spanish officials is no doubt a purely selfish one. The tourist is charged a fee of four dollars for *viséing* his passport, to enter the port of Havana, and the same when he leaves the island.

Our party of five paid a tax of forty dollars for the privilege of treading the streets of their dirty city. It proved a great bother, too; for neither Karzy, Moses, nor Mr. Garland were provided with passports from our government at the time, and to get them from Washington would have required at least two weeks' time. In this

MOUTH OF THE MISSISSIPPI RIVER.

dilemma we hit on the expedient of getting papers which answered as passports from the mayor of New Orleans, who is empowered to issue such when the parties are fully identified before him. A blank is provided, which the applicant fills out, as to the place and date of his birth, his height, complexion, and general *tout ensemble*. This he must solemnly swear to before a notary public, — even to the length of his nose and the size of his mouth! We had a jolly time getting out these documents, and nearly frightened Karzy into abandoning the voyage by assuring him that he had sworn to a nose an inch too short! — that the inquisitive Dons would at once detect the fraud and shut him up in *El Moro!*

The voyage down the Mississippi to the Gulf of Mexico gave us an opportunity to see the celebrated Eads jetties at the mouth of the

JACKSONVILLE, FLORIDA.

great river, where, by narrowing the channel, by means of dikes of stone and wicker, the depth of water on the "bar" has been increased from fifteen to twenty-six feet. Much has been said and written as to the success of these jetties. At present there can be no doubt that they have accomplished what was claimed for them in advance. Steamers of twenty-five feet draught can now enter and leave the port of New Orleans.

The steamers for Havana touch both at Cedar Keys and Key West, Florida. At the latter place we passed New Year's Day amidst a profusion of flowers and all tropic fruits. From the former point we made a flying visit to Jacksonville, and saw something of the proposed route of the new ship-canal designed to connect the Gulf of Mexico with the Atlantic coast of Florida.

So much has been said and printed of the proposed Panama canal through the isthmus between North and South America, that our people have well-nigh forgotten this great enterprise, nearer home, — one which will prove of scarcely less benefit to the commerce of the country.

Forgotten, we say — for this Florida canal is no new project. Nearly fifty years since the justly celebrated Commodore Maury earnestly advocated the building of a canal across Florida; and several Presidents, noticeably Presidents Pierce and Grant, in their messages strongly advised the building of such a canal by the government.

But it is the misfortune of all proposed public enterprises in this country, whether useful or not, to be indiscriminately and bitterly opposed by the party not in power, so that even needed enterprises are not undertaken.

A glance at the map of Florida will show the importance of such a canal to our domestic commerce, which is yearly increasing from Texas. And it will be a surprise to most persons to know that, according to the estimate of the New York Board of Trade, the amount of traffic which annually passes round the southern point of Florida into the Gulf of Mexico is three times that which passes through the famous Suez canal, connecting the Mediterranean and Red Seas.

Nor is there any doubt that shippers and ship-owners will gladly patronize the new canal. It will save, for vessels sailing for the mouth of the Mississippi and the Texas coast, fully eight hundred miles of navigation, and that too of the most dangerous navigation in the world. The loss of property by wrecks along the Florida coast and about its southern keys has been estimated at five million dollars annually, averaging thus for twenty-five years. It is reckoned that the canal will lower insurance rates two per cent on all consign-

ST. AUGUSTINE.

ments and shipping passing through it, and effect a more than corresponding reduction in freights.

The estimated cost of digging the canal is twenty millions. A company representing this amount, and more if necessary, has been recently organized in New York, and work will probably begin during the present year.

The line of the proposed canal extends from near Jacksonville, on the St. Johns River, directly across the State, to a point near the mouth of the Suwanee. The distance is about sixty miles.

CHAPTER IV.

IN LA HABANA. — GETTING ASHORE. — RAG MONEY. — LA CASA DE CORREOS. — ODOR DEL PAIS. — SPANISH ARCHITECTURE. — CUBAN OXEN. — LOTTERY TICKETS. — MOSES' TROUBLES. — STREET THIEVES. — OUR LODGINGS. — ABOUT TOWN.

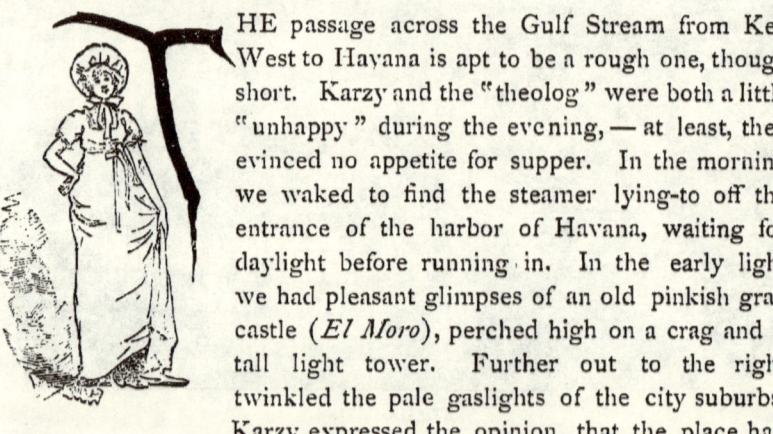

THE passage across the Gulf Stream from Key West to Havana is apt to be a rough one, though short. Karzy and the "theolog" were both a little "unhappy" during the evening, — at least, they evinced no appetite for supper. In the morning we waked to find the steamer lying-to off the entrance of the harbor of Havana, waiting for daylight before running in. In the early light we had pleasant glimpses of an old pinkish gray castle (*El Moro*), perched high on a crag and a tall light tower. Further out to the right twinkled the pale gaslights of the city suburbs. Karzy expressed the opinion that the place had "a mediæval look;" but thus far his ideas of mediæval objects have been drawn from books merely.

As soon as it was fairly light we steamed in past the Moro, entering a narrow cleft in the rough coralline coast, lined along with batteries. It is a tortuous entrance betwixt ugly reefs, but opens into a handsome, though small bay, encircled by green hills on one side and the city on the other.

But, though in harbor, we were not ashore. The steamer does not come to a pier, but drops her anchor out in the bay, there to wait the

HAVANA.

pleasure of the Spanish authorities. Two or three boats with rowers and officers in the uniform of the *Aduána* (Custom-House) soon put off, however, and with them numerous watermen in their boats, with couriers from the hotels, who, after the manner of their genus, raise a loud competitive clamor.

The watermen pull you ashore to the Custom-House, where you may wait an hour for your trunks to be inspected and your passport certified ere taking a coach for a hotel or your lodgings; if to a hotel you are there charged a fee of two dollars *oro* (gold) for "passport," which in this case means getting you ashore; and here it may be well to state that the terms of all the good hotels here are four dollars per day, gold, or about twice that sum in the depreciated paper money of Cuba. But it is a comfort to know that a "greenback" is worth here a little more than even Spanish gold.

Naturally one of the first places we went to was the post-office. It is down at the quay next to the *Aduána*, — a dingy, nondescript stone structure, over one of the portals to which are the words *Casa de Correos* (the House of Mails). The interior arrangements of this establishment are such as to defy alike description and the comprehension of a stranger. To any one needing to visit it, allow us to suggest the employment of an intelligent interpreter in advance; he and every other resource will be needed before you can get a letter out of the concern. Take along your passport, too, and as many of your personal friends as can be secured for the trip. Better still, never go there at all, but by well-written or printed directions, certificates, etc, contrive to have your letters sent to your hotel, or lodgings. But feel no surprise if you receive no letters, *much less newspapers;* and enjoin your friends at home to feel no alarm if they get no letters from you while in Cuba. If a mail-steamer is to leave on Thursday, post your letters for it Tuesday. This is a *mañana* country.

All letters received here not directed to street and number, instead of being put in an alphabetically arranged stand, are piled into a big drawer or box, to the number of twelve or fifteen thousand. Looking for one is a long business; and how carefully the indolent clerks examine the box may be conjectured. If your letters from home have on them a three-cent stamp only, you are charged twenty cents in currency, extra, on taking them. If a letter-carrier brings them he may charge more. Apparently the letter-carriers make what they can in such cases. People who shriek "corruption!" at home should see how public business is done in Cuba, under the present *régime*. "The bars are all down" here now. If you want anything done you must pay for it, and drive as good a bargain as you can.

As in Mexico, so here, one of the first things that impresses the American tourist, is the "odor of the country." It is everywhere, and in some spots it is awful! The old town, or that part formerly enclosed within the city walls, is a dirty place, with streets scarcely twenty feet wide, and sidewalks eighteen inches. Indeed, there is but one decent street in the city, — the Prado. And yet, despite these faults, Havana is a rather pretty city. At first view, it seemed to us a very white town, in contrast with the red brickwork of Northern cities. Everywhere the edifices and shops are white or perhaps light-pink, straw color, or light blue; and these colors are much heightened by the scorching brightness of the sun. It is well to have a pair of blue spectacles.

Then, from noting the color of the buildings, the eye comes to notice the marked difference in the style of architecture. Few edifices, public or private, are more than two stories in height; yet they look spacious, almost palatial. The most are built of stone or marble, very few brick, with walls which in the United States would be deemed immensely thick. The infrequency of fires and the very small losses thereby are easily understood, — there is little or no woodwork; and when we consider the terrific losses by fire at home, the idea suggests itself that this may be the better style of architecture.

AVENUE OF PALMS.

In the narrow streets, one meets cart after cart, piled high with bales of tobacco leaf, drawn by oxen. Much of the trucking is done by these patient creatures, which draw by a heavy yoke made fast to the massive tongue of the cart and bound to the foreheads of the poor brutes which thus push the load with their heads, instead of their shoulders, as in the United States. Each ox has a ring, or at least a hole, through his nostril, to which are attached strong rope reins; with these the driver on his cart directs their movements, not omitting the use of a long goad, armed with a sharp spike. Moses feelingly remarks that if the doctrine of *transmigration* be true, he sincerely hopes that he may not become an ox in Cuba — or a little coach-horse, either.

About the first person we ran against on stepping forth from the hotel after breakfast was a man who had sundry slips of paper in his fingers, and who saluted us with a dreary cry of, —

"*Veinte cinco mil pesos mañana!*"

"*Qué dices?*" (What do you say), demanded Karzy.

The fellow rattled off a long string of hazy Spanish, amidst which we caught on the word *loteria*. Havana is the paradise of lotteries, — lotteries every week. The venders of tickets bore you at every turn and corner. "*Mañana por la mañana ciento mil pesos!*"

Sit down on the settees in front of the hotel or at the "Place of Arms," and an endless procession of these persistent vagabonds, each with his doleful cry, will file past you and thrust the abominable little dog-eared billets in your face: "*Cinquenta mil pesos, señor!*" Moses had resort to his Spanish phrase-book, and extracted from it the words *Sega derecho*, the nearest approximation to "git!" which the Spanish language could furnish him. This he fired off continually at the *loteria* venders with an energy which often quite paralyzed them.

But the Spanish does not half express what struggles for utterance in Moses' bosom, particularly when a whole drove of beggars gets after him with their distracting whine of, "*Pobrecito! Pobre! pobre!*"

"It's against the law to stamp on them," he sighed. "If only the rascals knew God's own language I could make them scatter. But when I say 'Clear out!' they come the snugger."

By God's own language Moses means English — such as they speak in Indiana.

At breakfast, at the hotel, Moses called out imperatively for beefsteak.

"*Con mucho gusto*, señor" (With much pleasure), said the waiter.

"No, no!" exclaimed Moses, "not with *mucho gusto*. I want potatoes with it!"

"*Si señor, papas*," (potatoes), responded the waiter.

"Neither papas, nor grandpapas!" shouted Moses, "potatoes, I say!"

But the climax of our Hoosier comrade's mishaps came the fourth day of our stay in Havana, after we had taken lodgings in the house of an old Spanish captain, on the Prado, where by good luck we succeeded in establishing ourselves quite comfortably.

In Havana, and throughout Spanish America, the windows of the houses are protected on the outside by strong iron gratings, so that the robbery of a room through the window would seem a by no means easy matter to accomplish. Yet the street thieves here as elsewhere have proved fully equal to the obstacle.

Coming in tired and warm from a ride through the narrow streets, Moses threw open the inner shutters of his window, then sat down, and tipping back on his chair in American fashion with his head to the wall, presently fell in a drowse. His little *siesta* did not last for more than fifteen minutes, he thinks; but on awaking he immediately perceived that he had met with losses.

His boots, which he had pulled off and set by his side, had disappeared, likewise his sun umbrella. His travelling-bag, too, which was set closed and locked on a little table near by, stood gaping open; and from it his collar-box, cuff-box, handkerchief-box, night-shirt, and several pairs of hose, along with numerous other articles, were missing also.

MOSES' SIESTA.

As he had barred the folding-doors of his room before sitting down, and as the inner bar still remained in place, the very visible and extensive theft took the guise of presdigitry, difficult to explain. For the one window was guarded as usual with a grating, through which it would be impossible for an outsider to do more than thrust in his hand; and all the missing articles had lain fully two yards back from the window. The room was on the ground floor, however, and the window opened upon a little side-street not much frequented.

In great wrath, our comrade called in the *mozo* (house-servant), and summoned our host, to whom he explained by excited gestures and some few random Spanish words, the evil state of things.

Very gravely, and with that politeness that always characterizes your Spanish host, the old *señor* proceeded by signs to express his regrets and explain it all.

Gaucho, ladron, gauchito, largo baston, engauchar, gatada,— words which, well illustrated by signs and movements, portrayed to our indignant friend, that the *picaroz* (street rogues) have little hooks on long sticks with which they reach in betwixt the iron bars and successfully plunder a room, drawing out the articles one by one, and even turning the keys of trunks and wardrobes. In fact, these rogues,— often little black boys,— if unmolested, will in a few minutes completely despoil a room; and from some current stories which we heard of their skill I fancy that our comrade was rather fortunate in not having his coat unbuttoned and his pocket-book *hooked!* hooked, indeed!

It is a mistake for tourists at Havana, or in any other country which they really wish to see or learn anything of, to remain at the hotels. First-class hotels are so cosmopolitan in character, and so much alike the world over, that life in one, for more than a day or two, grows inexpressibly dreary. We were fortunate enough to obtain lodgings in a private family, where we had cool rooms, decent beds,— decent for Cuba,— and a very good table. In Cuba one must not look for a *colchon* (mattress) on his bed. We were **told** in advance that we should find no good beef. As a matter of fact, we found the beef excellent; nor was the *mantequilla* (butter) so bad as it had been pictured; it was not " gilt-edged," but fairly good. In addition to our other comforts, we had, in our old Spanish captain, a most enjoyable host, who spent hours trying to teach us his language — and all, as some may like to know, for twelve dollars per week. From this haven of comfort, which very soon came to seem like home, we went forth daily, to see the city, making excursions to Matanzas, Vedado Guines, and many other points, visiting the neighboring *ingenios* (sugar-plantations), the suburban villa and gardens of the Captain-General, and the grim old fortress across the bay.

CHAPTER V.

A PRIMITIVE MILK-CART. — KARZY'S TOOTHACHE. — HE GOES IN SEARCH OF A DENTISTA. — DENTIST'S FEES IN HAVANA. — THE HORSE BATHS. — HARBOR SHARKS. — AN INCIDENT — "UN TIBURON." — WAYSIDE "JOHNS." — THE GRAVE OF COLON.

MILK, called for by many names in many lands, is an article of food everywhere sold, and various indeed are the kinds of milk-carts in which it is peddled out.

The express-wagon with its load of tin cans, so familiar an object in our Northern cities, is a sufficiently business-like contrivance to suit the most utilitarian ideas.

In New Orleans, the milk-cart is a more picturesque vehicle, being a quaint little two-wheeled gig with a pair of urn-like cans, often ornamented with a fancy cap in brass, in front. Each can has a spigot and a measure chained to it, and both do not contain more than seven or eight gallons. Behind the cans is the milkman's little seat, protected from the hot sun-rays by a slight cover; a very quaint old-time rig of those *bizarre* creole days which Mr. Cable has done so much to render interesting.

In Mexico, your milkman comes around and rides in at your front door with his cans bagged up in coarse cloth and slung across the back of a sorry little *burro* (donkey), while he sits triumphantly perched on a pad betwixt them, lazily crying out, "*Leche, leche fresca!*"

HAVANA.

In the streets of Havana, the backs of the donkeys, mules, and little horses also serve as milk-carts, save where the milkman makes a still shorter cut at business, and drives the *vacas* (cows) themselves round to the doors, where he milks the universal fluid into your own quart dish, to suit your pleasure. This method has at least the advantage of relieving him of the temptation to water his milk. We commend it to all those dispensers of lacteal aliment in our Northern cities who feel themselves aggrieved by unjust suspicions; it is a method that admits of no aspersions.

MILK-CART.

At our house in Havana there used to come, every morning, a large *vaca*, — looking very much like one of the largest Jerseys, though of Cuban breed, — bringing her own milk in an odd-shaped can hanging on one side of her back, balanced on the other side by a roll of sweet cane stalks, — this latter provision looking much like a luncheon for the trip. Behind her toddled her little calf, with his nose securely trussed up to prevent his injudicious inroads upon the stock in trade. And still further behind came a young negro, whose humble cry of "*Leche, leche, veinte centavos el vaso!*" was at first our only key to this business.

The idea of a cow going about peddling her own milk, was so amusing to Karzy that he used to get up every morning at seven o'clock to look out and laugh at the spectacle.

"It is like these lazy fellows!" he would exclaim. "I would not be surprised to see that poor cow come along bringing the veal of her calf to-morrow!"

Veinte centavos (twenty cents) for a glass of milk! The Spanish captain with whom we lodged was obliged to pay eighty cents paper (about forty-three cents gold) a quart for the milk which he offered us as a luxury (and no wonder) for our coffee. Some American milkmen might do well to settle in the suburbs of Havana; or, perhaps ere long, some enterprising fellow in the North may send milk here by steamer in sealed cans packed in ice. There ought to be a fortune in that venture.

Havana, too, should be a good city for some of our numerous young American dentists to settle in. We judge so, — at least from an experience of Karzy's, which he had best be permitted to tell in his own way, as follows: —

"A few weeks ago, while at Havana, it was my misfortune to be overtaken by that old, old malady, toothache, or, in the language of the country, *dolor de muelas.*

"And it was very much *dolor*, indeed!

"But the tooth was a good and a serviceable one, or, at least, had been so. I disliked to part with it. Three days we strove together. One grieves to part from old friends, even when their behavior has of late become outrageous; for we cling to the good there was formerly in them.

CUBAN SCENERY.

"But the case grew hopeless. Forbearance ceased utterly to be a virtue, — rather a disgrace. I arose very early, — early for Havana, nine o'clock, — and sallied desperately forth to find a dentist, *ahora*, instantly.

"Near the *Hotel Pasaje* (pronounced pah-sah'-hee) I discovered a sign, —

> DENTISTA
>
> CIRJURIA-DENTAL.

which *dolor de muelas* enabled me to translate as *dentist* and *dental surgery*. Entering beneath a high-arched portal, and climbing a lofty stairway, I found myself in a spacious anteroom, with brilliantly stained windows, where sat two black mustachioed *señors*, who received me with grave politeness. One was in uniform, and wore a sword; but this, in Havana, is not unusual. At least every second man you meet is in uniform, and many of them carry not only a sword, but a revolver and a musket with a sabre bayonet, and would no doubt carry a cannon, but for the weight. Soldiers, everywhere soldiers. *Todos soldados!* Since the Cuban rebellion, Spain keeps a garrison of at least thirty thousand in Havana alone.

I was asked to sit down to wait my turn, as I succeeded in comprehending: a young *señorita* was ahead of me as a candidate for the operation of *estraccion de una muela*, — three *muelas*, in fact. I waited ten minutes, perhaps, encouraged and strengthened in my purpose by the terrific screams of the *señorita* upon whom *estraccion* was in progress, in the room beyond.

"At length the *señors* of the anteroom rose and ushered me into the *salon de estraccion*, where I found the operator, an alert young gentleman of twenty-three or four, who said, 'I spik Ingles; I was catorçe year in Nueva York.'

"Thus encouraged, I said, 'I wish to have a tooth extracted. It is the extreme back tooth of the lower jaw, upon the left side.'

"But this was not the kind of 'Inglis' which the operator 'spik,' evidently, and we made no apparent progress with each other, until I opened my mouth, and with my finger carefully indicated (for I wanted no mistakes made) the exact tooth which I wished to part company with. My new friend then got to work, and performed his painful offices without loss of time and in good style, so far as I observed.

"'And now the fee?' I said, rising. '*Que precio?*'

"'*Cinco pesos*, — fife tollar,' was the reply.

"This is about two dollars seventy cents in gold for a single *estraccion*, and I am told that some *dentistas* here charge four dollars, gold, for the same brief service."

Throughout the city, the horses, particularly the poor little horses which run up and down all day long, drawing the hundreds of streetcoaches, have a hot and hard lot; but every morning the most of them are permitted to enjoy a luxury unknown to Northern horses, — a bath in the sea.

Down at the end of the Prado, the chief avenue for driving and walking, where this fine broad avenue opens out upon the entrance to the harbor, there is a favorable place for these horse-baths; and here, from seven to ten o'clock in the morning, long files of horses — the halter of each tied to the tail of the next in advance, and the foremost ridden by a negro *cochero* — may be seen trooping into the cool water. It is a picturesque sight, and a very picturesque place, to stand by the parapet, just beyond the great Presidio. Directly across the narrow entrance to the port (no more than two hundred metres in breadth) tower the yellow and white walls of El Moro and the lighthouse. Out past it the shining waters of the gulf brighten and glow in the morning sunshine. Back to the right opens the fine haven full of shipping, long black and red steamers (*vapores*), and one or two fine ironclad rams moored to red buoys; a won-

A TROPICAL SCENE.

derfully good harbor, rent by nature into the solid ledges of this rocky coast.

The horses love the bath. It is the one bit of luxury in all their hard lives. They are allowed to remain in the water fifteen minutes or more. Some will be seen to lie down in it, regardless of their noses. Others stand with raised heads, the wavelets just breaking over their backs. Fine spans belonging to the Spanish magnates

HORSES BATHING.

are led in and groomed in the water for a long time, the black *cochero* talking lovingly to them all the while. Some very handsome horses from the United States are sold here to the wealthy classes. In the handsome marble house of a grandee you will see three or four tall, sleek, splendidly-lodged horses and several fine carriages on the first floor, while the family live up stairs.

The native horses and mules are all sorry little animals of very poor paces. They seem loath to come out of the cool water to begin their day of toil; but standing in the water, their enjoyment is a pleasant thing to see. We went morning after morning to watch them, and at length we witnessed a far livelier scene there.

The harbor of Havana, from time immemorial, has been infested by sharks, some of them of very large size. These have never been molested, since they act as scavengers for refuse meat and other unsavory matters which might otherwise contaminate the basin. Nevertheless, it might be a serious matter to tumble overboard from a boat, if some of these white-bellied gentry chance to be cruising near by. An incident is told of an American captain of a bark, who chanced to be in port some years ago, when Havana was a more lawless place than at present.

The captain, a New Englander, had concluded his business on shore late one afternoon, and going down to the quay, stepped into a waterman's boat and bade the man take him off to his vessel, which lay out in the harbor.

He had, as the result of his trading in port, a heavy bag of silver dollars, which he placed by his side in the stern of the boat. It was getting dusk, and when they were about half way off to the bark, the boatman, a dark-visaged, brawny fellow, quietly unshipped his oars, and drawing a long gleaming sheath-knife from a belt beneath his open shirt, sprang upon the American to murder him.

The captain was unarmed, but seeing the man's movement, he jumped up from his seat, and at the same time gave so convulsive a jerk at the pintle, or handle of the rudder, that it came off in his hand, and he thus most unexpectedly found himself in possession of a stick a yard long and as thick as his arm. The would-be-assassin raised his knife to strike, but ere his arm could descend, the pintle-stick descended on his skull with such force as to tumble him at full length backwards in the bottom of his boat. But as he showed signs of getting up, the captain seized him by the legs and threw him overboard, thinking he could best make terms with so murderous a rascal outside the boat. His body had hardly struck the water, however, when our American saw, to his horror, a huge shark rise close along-

ATTEMPTED ASSASINATION.

side. Slowly turning up ten or twelve feet of white belly in the twilight, the *tiburon* paid his respects to the *picarro* waterman, whom he took in charge without comments or trouble of police.

Occasionally a shark, poising further out in the channel, will make a sudden rush at the horses or at the *cocheros* in the waters.

Upon the morning above alluded to there arose a sudden cry of, —

"*Un tiburon! Un tiburon!*"

And out where a long file of horses were moving slowly, up to their backs, we saw one kicking, plunging, squealing.

The animal fell and went under. In an instant the whole troop was in disorder, all making frantic plunges toward the shore.

In a minute the whole place was astir. From all sides came running watermen, soldiers, police, slaves, cocheros, — everybody! And such a babel of shouts arose as even to drown the tremendous squeals of the poor horse as his head struggled up to the surface.

Boats put out, the watermen whooping and striking the water heavily with the flat of their long oars. And either alarmed by the noise, or because he had found the horse's legs a less palatable morsel than he had anticipated, the *tiburon* let go his hold and made off.

The horse was drawn out and led limping off to the stables, both its hind legs much lacerated.

Formerly, the Chinese were the most stay-at-home people in the world. They kept exclusively within their own land, and neither went abroad themselves nor would allow foreigners to come to them. This had been the national spirit for centuries.

But within the last half century, still more within the last ten years, a very marked and a very singular change has occurred in this ancient habit of life. The Chinese are now the greatest emigrants in the world. Even the globe-tramping Irishman is distanced at length.

Travel where you will, whether to the icy mountain fastnesses of British Columbia, or the mangrove swamps of Honduras; to the West Indies, Brazil, or some unpronounceable city of Cossacks, the odds are, that the first hour of your arrival will be rendered homelike by a glimpse of "John's" tunic, serious simple face, and laced up pig-tail, moving soberly up a street, or round a corner.

And everywhere, in all tongues, the same cry is raised against him: "He works all the time, gets all he can for it, spends nothing, and departing leaves nothing behind him, — not even his bones."

Such economy is not popular. The world seems to prefer the Irishman, — who works as little as he can, spends all he gets, begs, tramps, and leaves his body to be buried *in situ*, at the expense of the town.

At heart, we find poor brother "John" much like all the rest of us. We smile at his ever-serious phiz and his carefully-treasured up pig-tail. But this pig-tail he is compelled by law to keep; and which of us who had mortgaged his father and mother (a mortgage which, if foreclosed, would assign them to slavery) to get money to go into a distant land, there to brave all the uncertainties and hardships of a life of toil among foreigners, — which of us, I repeat, under such hard lines, would not look serious? Should we not be apt to be diligent, saving, and inclined to keep what we could?

Of all the foreign lands into which "John" wanders, seeking for either fame or fortune, the most luckless place in all the world, perhaps, at present is Cuba. For while in most lands times are now fairly good,

IN EVERY LAND.

here a blight has fallen. Times are dull, inexpressibly dull, and all the "Johns" here are stranded, — stuck fast. The poor fellows cannot even scrape together enough of the depreciated paper to get away on. It is of no use, either, for a Chinaman to go home unless he has earned money; so here they are, as forlorn and as utterly "broke" a class of beings as can well be pictured. The habitual seriousness of their faces has here taken on a shade of gloom not seen in other cities. But they never loaf; even when there is nothing to do, they go steadily and soberly up and down with an empty laundry basket. Here you will see one selling a few bits of dusty candy. Presently one calls at the house with two or three Chinese pictures in cheap frames, for which he asks unheard-of prices, or perhaps he has a few odd Chinese articles which it is easy to see are, or were, his private personal property. It has come to that with the poor boy. A few find work at breaking stone for the street in the Prado.

JOHN CHINAMAN.

But I cannot hear that they ever beg, though beggars are as common as dogs. They do not readily learn Spanish. Most of them know a little English, and brighten at the sound of an English word, as if it calls to mind better times in the States. To one breaking stone in the hot sun with a heavy hammer Moses said, "How do, John? You go to California?" The rare smile that lit up his sad face was a sight, indeed! But it soon faded out. "No got money," he replied, and shook his head.

How far off and how utterly hopeless must his Chinese home and all the dear objects there look to this poor world-waif!

And in that Chinese home what hopes may be hanging on this unpromising castaway!

Indeed, but for certain prejudices which we can hardly rise superior to, we should find the most genuine tragedies of the age in the homely affairs of these wayside "Johns."

An American is so accustomed to think of Columbus as the grand discoverer of the New World — his world — that for a moment he feels like resenting the exclusive claim of this not over-clean and badly-governed city of Havana to the guardianship of his ashes.

It seems odd to hear him spoken of as Colon, and find his grave in a Catholic church here. Columbus — or Cristobal Colon, as we must call him in Cuba — died in Santo Domingo, or Hayti; but his remains were subsequently removed to the Cathedral in Havana, where, beneath a pillar within the altar, they now repose. Properly proud are the Havanese Spanish of their great fellow-countryman by adoption, whose last resting-place is with them.

CHINESE AT HIS DEVOTIONS.

Beneath a rather doubtful bust of the great discoverer, a marble tablet, set in the pillar, is inscribed with the following characteristically Spanish epitaph in the old-time dialect of Castile: —

"*O, restos y ymagen del grande Colon! Mil siglos durad guardado en la urna y en la remembranza de nuestra nacion.*"

"O remains and likeness of great Columbus! Let a thousand

centuries hold thee guarded sacredly in thy urn and in the memory of our nation."

More correct to life, it is said, is the statue of Columbus in the *patio* of the captain-general's palace, a few squares away. Here his

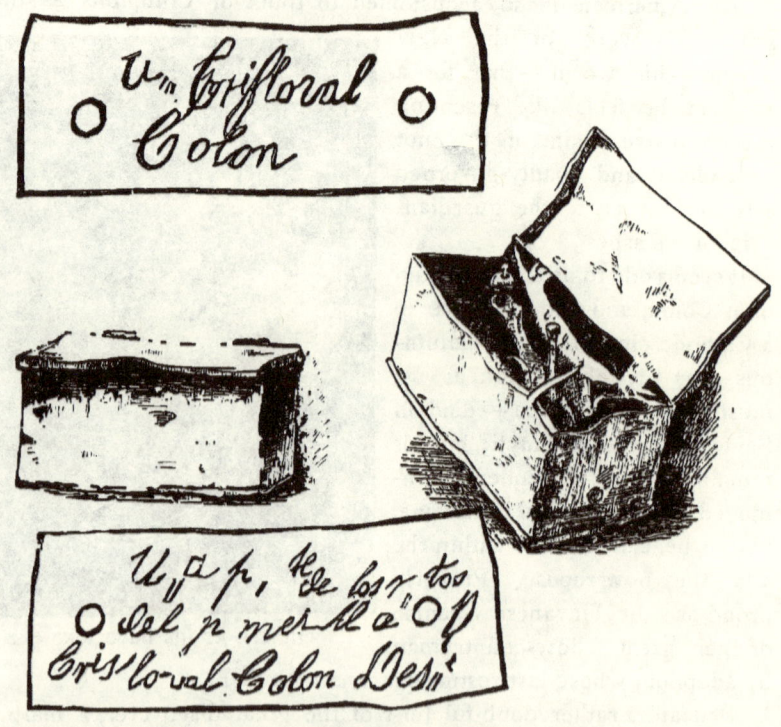

RELICS OF COLUMBUS.

hand points to a globe (that globe which he was persecuted for believing to be round and not flat!) and a chart. The head and face are those of a man forty-five or fifty years of age; and the countenance indicates a certain pathetic faith and purpose, half buried and struggling beneath tides on tides of trouble. One cannot for a moment look upon that face and believe that the life of this man was a happy one — rather that he suffered from first to last; from the day he first set forth to raise funds for his ridiculed expedition to that last hour in Santo Domingo, when his noble life expired beneath ingratitude and malice.

Such a face is a silent and lasting reproach to the age which it looked upon.

CHAPTER VI.

CARNIVAL. — A FIRE IN HAVANA. — ABOUT CUBA. — MATANZAS. — CUEVA DE BELLAMAR. — AT AN INGENIO. — CAPTURING A MAJA. — THE CUBAN WAR. — A TRAGIC INCIDENT. — IN AN OLD MOLASSES HOGSHEAD.

WE chanced to be in Havana during the carnival season, and witnessed the ludicrous turnouts and processions at the Prado on the three consecutive Sabbaths preceding Lent; but these carnival crazes have been so often depicted that the reader's good humor need not be taxed with the details of these masquerades.

On the night of the 30th of January we were witnesses of the great fire on the Prado, where a hundred and twenty firemen were disabled.

Fires are of rare occurrence in Havana. This one originated in an American livery stable, — a tinder-box, as usual, — and was thence communicated to some extensive lumber-yards.

In a Northern city such a "blaze" would be thought of no great consequence; but here it created a scene of terror and distress not easily imagined; and the *bomberos* (firemen), of feeble physique, and unused to such exertion, dropped down by the dozen. For a week little else than the fire and the "heroic" firemen were talked of throughout the city.

Previous to this, however, we had visited Guines and Matanzas, and at the latter city were present at the grand ball which concluded the International Exposition held there.

Of other Cuban towns and of Cuban scenery in general there is little need to make mention. Journeying in Cuba is a tiresome business at best, whether by rail or on horseback, unless, in the latter case, it is made during a few hours of the early morning, before the scorching heats of midday. The railway cars are all what we term at home second-class cars, with bad springs and hard seats. The windows are necessarily all open, and the dust, smoke, and heat are unusually troublesome.

The cave of Bellamar, near Matanzas, is, perhaps, the most wonderful natural curiosity of Cuba. And even after one has seen the Mammoth Cave of Kentucky and the great bat-caves of Texas, he will still find Bellamar worth a visit. It is situated two miles out of Matanzas — just a good early morning walk for an American, after coffee.

GATHERING PALMS.

Like nearly all the remarkable caverns of the world, this *cueva* is in a limestone foundation — a part of that odd, dome-shaped range which years ago our Northern skippers, voyaging to Cuba after molasses and rum, named the "Bread of Matanzas" (*El Pau de Matanzas*), because, seen from the sea, it resembles a row of bread-loaves.

The way to it lies beside the bay, then up a steep hill, with fine scenery on both sides; and the entrance to the cave is in the midst of a small clearing, on a perfectly flat limestone plateau.

They tell us that it was accidently discovered by a former owner who was breaking out stone for his lime-kiln. On a sudden the rock sank away beneath his blows, and he found, to his amazement, that he had a tremendous hole on his hands.

After a time he ventured down into it, and was astonished still more to find how large it was, and what beautiful stalactites hung from the roofs of the many "rooms" and passages. These, as in the great limestone caverns of the United States, are formed by the infiltration of the water through the strata of lime rock above. Many of these beautiful glistening marble icicles are not less than thirty feet in length. They stand singly and in groups, often fantastically twined together, some semi-transparent, some of a pinkish hue, others dead white.

Further on great areas of the roof sparkle with densely-packed spikelets, bright as glass. Wonderful is the variety and beauty of the different mazes of this dark labyrinth, — a beauty which the torches of the guide but dimly reveal.

Stein took the liberty of suggesting to the proprietor that an electric light would produce beautiful effects; but some American had already sold him a gasoline apparatus, which he had used for a time and taken out, because the smoke from it was ruining the stalactites, and he did not take kindly to the hint.

The various rooms and passages have been named, as in Mammoth Cave. We find the "*Catedral*," the "Rotunda," the "Devil's Mouth," the "*Bano de la Americana*,"—" Bath of the American Lady,"— so called because one of our fellow-countrywomen who visited the cave was so fascinated by the beauty of the room and the crystal purity of the pools of water on one side, beneath the stalactites, that she insisted on being left in it to take a bath.

IN THE CAVE.

Perchance she fancied that the fable of the fountain of youth might be true after all, and that this pool was the place of magic waters.

Then we come to the "Indian Woman's Path" and the "Hall of the Twelve Apostles," the "Grotto of the Monkey," and the "Señora's Boudoir," where we see, in pure white stone, the form of a lady.

These subterranean *salons* have been explored to a distance of a mile and a half from the entrance. The present owner has provided very comfortable and safe facilities for seeing the cave; and the price — one dollar — is by no means unreasonable.

Not so reasonable, however, are the charges of Matanzas *cocheros* for driving a visitor out to the cave; and we would respectfully hint to all tourists of an economical turn of mind, to imitate our example, and make the trip on foot between the hours of half past six and nine in the morning.

While stopping over night at an *ingenio* (sugar-mill) near Matanzas, we were awakened early in the morning by an uproarious outcry in a neighboring pig hovel, where were ten or twelve little porkers, not yet a month old; and immediately we heard the negroes shouting, —

"*Maja, Maja!*" (pronounced *mah-hah*).

"It is a great snake, — a pig-snake!" exclaimed the young engineer with whom we were stopping, and who had been engaged for some weeks at the *ingenio* putting in a *fornalla*, or furnace, for consuming the green *begasse* of the sugar-cane for fuel. "Come out, and we will see some fun!"

We threw on coats, hats, and boots, and hastening forth saw ten or a dozen negroes gathering round the pig hovel, some with *machetes* (cane-cutters), some with *fornalla* pokers, while others were bringing several of those large, long lines, such as the teamsters here pass through holes in the nostrils of the poor draught oxen to rein and guide them by.

The squeals had ceased, but the *maja* was still in the pig hovel; so, at least, we judged from the stealthy movements of the negroes, who were carefully pressing the gate together and stopping up several gaps in the palings with bits of board and thick banana stalks.

Then a great jabbering in their pigeon Spanish followed, — probably as to the best method of getting out the serpent. Seeing that they had hit on a plan, we stood and watched their motions. Two stalwart mulattoes took one of the long ropes and made an open noose at the middle of it. Another opened the gate of the hovel a little way, guarding the crack, however, with a piece of board. The two with the noose then fixed it with forked sticks in front of the crack of the gate, the bottom of it resting on the ground and covered with dust; the noose was, perhaps, a foot in diameter as it hung.

Their rope trap being at length placed to suit them, the two mulattoes took each an end of the rope, and standing opposite each other, forty feet apart, perhaps, signified to the others that they were ready.

The negro who was holding the board before the crack at the gate then cautiously slipped it away, and retired with speed, when *carramba!* all the others stationed with pokers and poles at the back of the hovel raised a simultaneous "*Hola!*" and beat upon the sides and eaves of the shed, making a frightful racket.

At the first note of the clamor, the *maja* — a great, dark, ash-colored snake — glided out through the noose at the crack of the gate, having a pig well down in his gullet.

At sight of him a yell rose, and the two mulattoes at the ends of the line jerked backward with all their force, drawing the noose tightly and catching the *maja* around the body at a point three or four feet back of his head. Six or eight others ran to help them pull the harder; and then the fun began in earnest!

The snake first spit out his pig; then began such a struggle for liberty as at once enlisted our full sympathies for him.

"Here is a Cuban patriot," exclaimed Stein, "with a rope round his neck, doing battle with ten Spaniards!"

At his first muscular bounce the *maja* landed himself a dozen feet clear of the gate, disclosing his entire length, — which was certainly not less than fourteen feet, and the reader can judge of the reptile's strength from the fact that in his bounds to and fro he pulled the negroes violently back and forth with the rope. His long tail cut the air like a cart-whip; and our friend, the engineer, assured us that a stroke of his tail across a man's stomach would be as fatal as a musket-shot.

With every spring the reptile expelled its breath with a shrill sound, and its black eyes grew livid with rage.

KILLING THE SNAKE.

The struggle continued for eight or ten minutes; and though the negroes had no great difficulty in holding the rope straight, and thus keeping the *maja* at a distance from their legs, yet the entire party were carried over nearly an acre of ground in the *melée*, knocking down a whole plat of tall bananas on the side of the *quinta*.

But numbers prevailed (as they did here in 1878). The tightly-drawn noose, backed by vigorous blows from pokers and poles, quelled the lithe *maja* at length; and half an hour later two negroes were busily engaged stripping off its skin, to be tanned for shoe leather.

Our engineer friend told us that he once saw one of these large *majas* chase a horse which had accidentally angered it by stumbling into its hole. The snake, darting out, struck the horse with its tail so heavy a blow that the animal uttered a loud squeal, and ran away; but the enraged *maja*, whirling rapidly along,— first from its head, then from its tail, — not only kept pace with the horse, but lashed it so furiously that my friend thinks the horse would have been killed, had it not run into a shed, where several negroes came to its relief.

This incident may call to mind some of the wonderful accounts which we occasionally hear of the strength and swiftness of large black snakes in the United States.

While in Cuba we heard a great deal of the late war there, or "the great insurrection," as the Spaniards term it, which raged in the eastern districts for eight years prior to 1878, and which reduced large and previously prosperous sections of the island to the condition of a desert.

Mr. A——, one of Stein's acquaintances at Havana — an American who fought in the patriot army throughout the long, bitter, and hopeless struggle for Cuban independence — told him many incidents of the war, two of which he has written out, and contributes them to our book.

A TRAGIC INCIDENT.

Sitting on a block of limestone which the workmen with their double-faced axes had just squared down for the new market-house, I saw a hideous object, yet in human shape; so hideous that I shrink from describing it, and must search for softening words, lest I shock the reader. It was the form of a negro, shrivelled and clad in two rags which held the place of drawers and shirt. Where should have been the eyes were two deep sightless pits, frightfully livid and broken, like what my boyish fancy used to portray in the forehead of Polyphemus after that Ulysses had bored out the gigantic eye.

Ears it had none; — and what a strange, almost terrific aspect the human head has without the ears! Instead were two blood-red scars where they had been cut away. The face, the exposed breast, and the arms were literally seamed and scored with deep lines, the paths of gaping sabre wounds. Involuntarily I closed my eyes to pass; I had heard of beggars who in the interest of their trade with human sympathy had mutilated themselves. But my Cuban friend laid a hand upon my arm, and with a gesture almost pathetic, I thought, said to me softly, "Put a little money in his hand and say cheerfully, *Buenas tardes, Florencio!*" and he set the example himself, — a rather lavish one, for I saw that he slipped a paper dollar into the terrible hand of the sightless anatomy.

I felt a little surprised. Ordinarily my friend paid little attention to beggars; for here in Havana beggars of all degrees of human decrepitude and malformation are as plenty as are buzzards.

Presently, as we went out into the Prado, he said, "That poor wretch was not a professional beggar, like the most of them. He is a hero, — as true, faithful a fellow as ever breathed, and worthy of all any one can give him. You saw how he was chopped to pieces. The Spaniards did that because he wouldn't turn traitor to us in the war. It is one of our Cuban tragedies. Tragedies were plenty here from 1870 to 1877; that struggle which the world calls the Cuban insurrection. No history of our war has ever been written, and none save some of those who fought it through to the last bitter hour of defeat and prison bars know what we suffered here. Cuba, which so ardently desired to be a free state, like the other fair lands of the New World, lies conquered; her business ruined, her plantations a wreck, her money a mass of dirty depreciated paper rags that the very beggars turn up their noses at, and everywhere troops, troops, soldiers, soldiers, which we are taxed to the earth to support, — to hold us in submission. Bitter, indeed, is the fate of that country which tries to be free and fails. Had we succeeded in 1870, as we nearly did, how different would be the condition of Cuba to-day! The world would now call us patriots and illustrious instead of conquered *rebels!*

"That poor negro was a slave on one of the sugar-plantations out near Porto Principe. The place is a wreck now, a desert; but in 1870 it was a fine estate, where one of my personal friends — whose name I must withhold — had recently put in machinery for crushing cane and boiling molasses, to the value of a hundred thousand *pesos* (dollars). But he was an ardent patriot, and loved Cuba and her freedom better than his business. By every means, personally and by the aid of his fortune, he worked for the public liberty, both in Havana and in New York, to secure our recognition as belligerents and to enlist volunteers in the

North to fight the Spanish in the field. In consequence of his exertions he was soon a marked man — marked by the government for execution when caught. This was as late as 1874, after the Cubans had emancipated their slaves as a war measure, and hoped that they would fight with them against the common enemy. As might have been foreseen, however, the most of them went their ways, caring very little for Cuban independence, and in some cases even taking up arms against us. One of my friend's blacks, however (this same Florencio), did not leave the *ingenio*, but remained looking after the property during his former master's many absences, and attending to his comforts when at intervals he returned for a few days.

It chanced that my friend had been on a secret mission to Havana, where he was kept concealed in the house of a compatriot for a number of days — entering and leaving the city by night along dark alleys, and journeying across the country by routes which were known to him from boyhood, but with which the enemy's *guardias* were unfamiliar. This, indeed, was but one of many such trips in behalf of our lost cause; and such was his knowledge of the country that hitherto he had been able to make them without discovery.

But on this occasion some spy or some traitor had given the Spanish the clue and put the soldiers on his track.

He had been at the *ingenio* no more than an hour when Florencio, who had gone out to the *quinta* to gather a bunch of *plantanos* (bananas), came hurriedly back into the engine-house of the *ingenio*, which my friend, in the general wreck of his household goods, occupied as a sleeping-room and hiding-place: "*Por amor de cielo, maestro!*" he exclaimed, "*Los Soldados!*" "For the love of Heaven, master, the soldiers are here!"

Stepping to the window, my friend saw that Florencio's warning was but too true. A troop of cavalry was riding furiously up to the *ingenio*, deploying as they came on to throw a cordon of men round the mill.

To escape by flight was impossible, and he well knew what capture meant; yet my friend's coolness did not forsake him.

"Close the shutters," he said to the negro; "and bar the door, but open it when they summon you. Say that I have gone. They will not hurt you, I think."

The furnace of the engine-room was one of those broad-mouthed *fornallas* for consuming the green *begasse* of the sugar-cane as fuel. Into this fire-box my friend crept, and, regardless of soot and dust, made his way up the inside of the narrow brick flue to a kind of widened jog, or jamb in the brick work, where he was able to stand out of sight, even to one looking up the flue from inside the fire-box. Florencio had closed the furnace door behind him on the instant.

Scarcely had he gained his perch on the jamb when, without waiting to knock, or order the door opened, the soldiers staved it in with the tongue of an old cane cart which lay in the yard; and then confusedly (for the iron and brick of the *fornalla* muffled the sounds) my friend heard himself peremptorily inquired for as a cursed *traidor* (traitor) by the captain of the troop.

Florencio replied that his master had been there, but had gone.

"*Perro negro!*" (black dog), shouted the officer, "Tell me where he is instantly, or I will have you flayed alive!"

Florencio answered merely that he had nothing to tell; that his master had gone.

The soldiers then searched the engine-house and all the other buildings of the mill. They even looked into the fire-box of the *fornalla*, and stirred up the heaps of cinders at the bottom of it.

Following this, my friend again heard the officer order Florencio to tell where his master had gone; but the faithful fellow persistently replied that he had nothing further to tell.

Presently the soldiers took him out into the yard and bound him to a palm trunk. Repeatedly then, for the space of an hour, which seemed an age to my endangered friend, he heard them threatening Florencio at intervals. Several times, too, he thought that he heard the poor fellow cry out; and he had no doubt that they were beating him, or pricking him with their swords. But he had little idea that they were inflicting upon him the horrible tortures which the event showed, else — as he has often declared to me with tears in his eyes — he would have come out and surrendered rather than have allowed it.

And that the negro should have endured such agony without shrieking is one of the strongest proofs of his fidelity and his nerve. They literally cut the flesh from his bones. Not a patch of his skin remained which was not gashed with their sabres. One by one they cut off every toe, and as a crowning act of torture, they dug out the poor faithful slave's eyes, and cutting off his ears, crammed them into his mouth!

Such cruelties are almost too horrible to be believed; and no doubt can exist that the wretches who had the heart to perpetrate such horrors upon a fellow-being were the true descendants of the *inquisitors* who, three centuries ago, made the Christian religion the excuse for outrages upon humanity, such as the world to that time, through ages of savagery and heathenism, had never dreamed of.

In the name of humanity, I ask the enlightened world, how long should this fair island of Cuba remain in the clutches of such men?

After a time the troop rode away; and my friend presumed that they had taken Florencio with them; for he heard nothing of him.

A TRAGIC INCIDENT.

After it had grown dark, he ventured to creep down from out the *fornalla*, when he found his poor servant in a swoon, still hanging by the rope to the palm trunk.

Life was not extinct, however, and toward morning the poor creature revived and faintly spoke his master's name.

My friend says that those few words from him were the saddest, most reproachful, yet the sweetest music he ever heard.

He nursed him there for two months, and afterwards hired a negro to wait upon him constantly.

Eighteen months later my friend fell in one of our hopeless battles, and Florencio at length found his way to Havana.

You can understand why it is that I never pass the poor fellow by. In the name of Cuba's lost liberty, I always give him something; and I would divide my last dollar with him rather than see him suffer further.

IN AN OLD MOLASSES HOGSHEAD.

It was a hot night even for Cuba, and April nights in this tropic island are not commonly suggestive of icebergs.

This was in 1873, during the very worst and bloodiest times of the Cuban insurrection, "when war to the knife and no prisoners" had begun in dire earnest on both sides. For the government troops were accustomed to shoot down a "patriot" at sight, armed or unarmed; and on our side the volunteers were not slow to sanguinary reprisals upon any of the hated Spanish *soldados* who showed their heads in the interior about Porto Principe.

Those were the times when Cuban planters were destroying their own plantations, slaughtering their cattle rather than let the government troops find food or a resting-place in the eastern districts; when the wells and springs were choked with dead carcasses, so that not a drop of good water should solace the enemy on his marches against us; when even the women watched all day in the tops of the ceiba trees to give us notice of the approach of the invaders, — women who, in their devotion to the cause of this fair island's liberty, were not less self-sacrificing than those of Carthage. Alas, that such devotion should have been in vain! But not in vain forever; Cuba will be free, — the patriotic fire and fervor in the hearts of her sons and daughters is not extinguished. Covered now, but hot and quick, it smoulders ready to break into flame when the favorable hour shall strike.

For three months our little company of forty-six men, under Captain Green, had been living as best we could in the *monte* to the southeast of Porto Principe; often in want of food, but ready to fight any detachment the Spanish General might send against us. That afternoon we had come out to Tunas, and there, just at nightfall, a negro from Porto Principe informed us that the enemy had taken the town, and had by a *rue-de-guerra* succeeded in surrounding a company of "patriots" at an *ingenio*, or sugar-mill, where they were defending themselves desperately.

But such rumors were everywhere rife then. The negroes were constantly spreading exciting news, and some of these latter were paid spies of the Spanish, who sought thus to draw us into ambuscades, and once or twice, in the case of our less cautious officers, had succeeded.

Nevertheless, the news made a flurry among the men, particularly the *Cubanos*, who were very mobile-tempered. There were eight of us Americans in the company, five of whom had served in the Civil War; and upon us our *capitan*, being an American himself, naturally relied.

"Most likely it's a lie, perhaps a trick," he said to us; "still we cannot tell; and I wish one of you boys would go down there and see what's up!"

The distance was twelve *leguas*, no pleasant trip hot and bootless. But Warren Robertson (afterwards killed at the *solado*) and myself stepped forward together.

"Thanks," said Captain Green. "I don't like to choose between you; snap up a *real!*"

We did so, and my choice of the head came up.

A decent horse and a negro guide were found for me in the hamlet; for though I had been across the country two or three times already I knew little of the various roads and devious *estradas* which it might be necessary to take, particularly by night.

When it had grown dark, not till then, I set off, keeping the black boy, who was mounted on a large mule, a little in advance, giving him plainly to understand that any attempt on his part to desert or play me a trick would surely draw a shot from my Winchester. These blacks were many of them great rascals; but they knew the country like a book, and it was when the enemy began to employ them as scouts that the greatest mischief was done us.

The night was hot, damp, and dark, — so dark that I could but faintly make out the ghostly white trunks of the palms which everywhere stud the half-cleared lands. The only sounds, save here and there the barking of dogs, were the chirrupings of the frogs, and now and then the screeches of parrots where a *maja* was trying to catch them. Once or twice we passed closely upon groups of negroes — *picaros* — out on their forays.

By four o'clock we had arrived among the *quintas* which skirt the town, and here I hitched up the animals, and then went on foot with the negro to the hut of a black man whom he knew, and who I surmised could tell the news, if there were any. Cautiously rousing out the black gardener, I elicited from him the intelligence that four *batallóns* of the enemy's infantry and a company of cavalry had entered the town the previous day, but that there had been no fight. Even as he was telling me this the morning bugles of the different *batallóns* began to sound up at the plaza.

The fellow evidently told the truth. If there had been a battle at that small town, he would have been sure to know it. Moreover, if treacherous, he seemed friendly, and gave us oranges and bread freely.

This being the state of affairs, I determined to retrace my steps and get away from the town a good bit before the sun had risen. We set off accordingly, and had ridden for an hour, perhaps, along the road we had come, — but very leisurely, for our animals were much fatigued, — when directly ahead I heard a loud "*Hola!*" and saw a squad of Spanish cavalry running upon us at a furious gallop.

The negro with whom I had conversed had probably gone on the instant of my departure and betrayed me in hope of a reward.

The black boy with me cried out in abject terror, and slipping off his mule took to the *guava* hedge; and not caring for a hand-to-hand conflict with eight or ten troopers, I wheeled through a gap in the hedge, on the other side, and rode for life through a field of young cane, keeping to cover of a row of palms.

Crack, crack, and *whiz, whiz, whiz*, went a half-dozen carbine shots past me. The rascals were hard after me, and my poor horse was already well used up. Beyond the cane was a belt of low orange trees, and through these I came plump down upon the bank of one of those deep, sluggish Cuban creeks, half choked with high, rank grass. There was no time for looking out a ford. I put my horse at it, and with the first spring he landed me in the middle of the stream, over his back in mud and water, and there stuck fast. I slid over his head and struggled to the further bank, wet to my skin and plastered with black mud. On that side were also orange trees; through them I ran, the water streaming off me, — stimulated by the crack of a carbine from behind, where a trooper had caught a glimpse of me. The orange orchard was perhaps two hundred meters in width, and from it I emerged at full run upon a deserted *ingenio*, where beneath the long storage shed my eye fell on thirty or forty hogsheads of molasses ranged in a row, on their sides, upon a platform against the back wall.

In such stress for life a person will sometimes have strangely quick, vivid thoughts. When a boy, far up North in my New England home, I had worked for three or four winters at making "shook," as we called it ; that is, riving and shaving red-oak staves for molasses hogsheads, which our Northern schooners, sailing to the West Indies after molasses, took thither with them, bound up in bundles, just as we made them in the woods.

In that moment of fear and desperation, no one can tell what a homelike feeling came to me from the sight of those oaken hogsheads. Two or three others, empty, one with one head out, lay about on the platform; and as my eye fell upon it a sudden thought — like a whispered word — flashed in my mind! 'T would be a bold trick. Dared I risk it! Once, years ago, when a boy playing at hide-and-seek in the old barn at home, I had hit on that same *ruse* to delude my play-fellows and succeeded completely. *I would risk it.*

All this passed through my mind, probably, in a single second of time.

As quickly did I act — rolling two of the full hogsheads at one end of the row back a little from the others, and introducing into the gap in the row the empty hogshead, with the open end turned next to the wall. Fortunately for my trick, this hogshead had the remaining outer head painted red, like the others in the row.

IN THE MUD AND WATER.

To toss my carbine into the well at the end of the shed, and slip my body down beside the wall, was but the work of another moment; and then by two or three vigorous pulls and hitches I contrived to work the cask (with myself in it) so far back that the open head could not readily be detected, even by one passing close to the row. *My* hogshead thus resembled the others so closely as not to be distinguished from them, unless it were moved.

Thus ensconced I drew my revolver, and waited the outcome of the adventure. A minute had not yet elapsed since I came out to the *ingenio*, yet I was none too soon. Scarcely had I got quiet in my hogshead when, with loud "*holas!*" and shouts of,—

"*Carramba!*"

"*Perro Americano!*" four or five of the troopers who had managed to get their horses through the creek came galloping up to the mill, followed by the others on foot — all wet and swearing as only such troopers can!

Through a tiny crack in the head of my cask I could catch glimpses of them. They had tracked me to the shed; and now I shuddered to see that they had detected my wet foot-prints on the platform itself. Surely they must find me now. Setting my teeth and grasping the butt of my pistol, I determined to sell my life at a good price; six of them should die with me, I vowed.

Shouting and cursing, they rushed along past the row of hogsheads, following my last tracks to the well. This they examined closely, and even threw down six or eight heavy stones, thinking, I presume, that I might be ducking under the water. Then they came back past the row of hogsheads, fuming and execrating me in stiffest phrase. One of them ran along on the top of the hogsheads, then came slowly back, actually standing for several seconds upon the *very cask in which I lay coiled!* Then they all hurried away to search the engine-house and other buildings of the *ingenio*. For fully half an hour I heard them rummaging and shouting. Twice their officer came back to the well; and the last time he had two of the men pitch down more and heavier stones, — seeming to be of the opinion that I must be down there. At length they went on, to search further, no doubt.

I kept close in my tub for an hour or two; then unable to bear the cramped position longer, I crept cautiously out and hid in the engine-house, and here I remained all day. When it was fairly dark I sallied forth, and getting a stick, climbed down into the well by the rod and pipe of the windmill pump, hoping to recover my carbine. But the rascals had buried it too deep beneath the stones which they had thrown down. I could not get it up, and, much to my chagrin, was obliged to leave it there.

Next I went out to the creek, thinking that if my horse was anywhere about I would again impress him into my service. But some one else had taken him, or he had gone away by himself. I was obliged to make my way back to Tunas on foot, *minus* my Winchester, — a serious loss at that time.

CHAPTER VII.

ON BOARD THE "CITY OF MERIDA." — TROPIC HEATS. — A "NORTHER." — ON THE GULF IN A TEMPEST. — SOME FEARS AND MUCH DISCOMFORT. — MOSES RESIGNED. — ORIZABA IN SIGHT. — VERA CRUZ.

ON the morning of the 18th of February the staunch old steamship "City of Merida" was lying off Frontera, in the Bay of Campeche. Like nearly all the gulf ports of Mexico, Frontera has no harbor, and all vessels coming here (including the New York, Havana, and Mexican mail steamers) anchor eight or ten miles off the shore, and trans-ship their cargoes into "lighters," which come out for it. It is a tedious process, and an entire day may be consumed unloading a few tons of freight.

The day was a hot one even for the Bay of Campeche, enclosed about by the *tierra caliente*. Not a breath of wind stirred the shining surface of the green sea; and under the awning of the after-deck it seemed as if our heads would burst from the sultry oppressiveness of the almost vertical sun-rays. We sighed for a breeze; just a breath, ever so little, would have been an unspeakable relief.

Twelve, one, two o'clock came. It was too hot to eat, well-nigh too hot to breathe. How the crew contrived to work, hoisting out freight, was a matter of astonishment. The very creak of the tackle-blocks was painful, and the ship's bells gave one a headache. Some of the Indians in the lighters lay asleep in the half shadow of the listless sails, and our fellow-traveller, Moses O——, tried to sleep in the shade of a deck-boat. Stein tried to read " Prescott's Conquest of Mexico," and Karzy essayed to fan himself with a " Seaside," which he had long ago given up trying to read.

Presently we became aware of a sudden and unusual stir aboard; the captain was seen to go hastily forward, the engineer to come rather quickly from his room. Then the second officer was heard ordering off the lighters; anon black smoke rolled up from the twin funnels.

"Something must be the matter with the barometer," remarked the old English passenger.

"A 'norther,' I reckon," observed the mahogany dealer.

"Well, a 'norther' wouldn't go so bad," said Moses, rolling out from the barren lee of his boat.

"Ah, the very name of it sounds sort of cool and refreshing," panted Karzy.

Still the sun poured, — *mucho calor!*

But twenty or thirty minutes later a dark, rough line was espied moving down across the glass-bright water far to the northward, and on the horizon in that quarter a single amber cloud had risen.

"There comes the breeze!" was the cry, and all got up and stood looking pantingly toward it.

The ruffled line of water bore down upon us, and, gentle as a zephyr at first, it flapped our heated awnings, — ah, how gratefully!

But the captain seemed to distrust it; the awnings were at once hauled off and stowed away. Everything, in fact, was lashed fast and made snug. Immediately the anchor was raised, and the old ship moved off under a full head of steam, not toward Vera Cruz, where she was due next morning, but to the northward, directly up into the Gulf.

Within an hour we all began to feel that it was getting fresh,—cold, in fact. Overcoats and thick caps came out; by sunset the ocean was really stormy and rough, and in the north and west a vast blue-black bank of clouds had risen, across which, in the twilight, played gleaming lines of lightening. Toward it, heading into the rising wind, the old steamer ploughed and plunged under full pressure of her screws.

The supper-table, hitherto so jolly a gathering-place, was strangely deserted to-night, the most of our friends appearing to have personal cares in their state-rooms.

By nine o'clock the sensation of heavy weather, not unattended with danger, had crept over all. The ship was rolling and pitching violently, and the wind, the "norther," how it howled and whistled! Ere long waves began to break over the bulwarks, and random *douches* of water to dash in at the state-room windows. Then came a fearful lurch, followed by a terriffic crash of crockery and glasses in the pantry, and a general upset of trunks and chairs, amidst the tumble and rumble of which there rose a wail of anguish, from all the afflicted.

The "fun" had begun.

To cross, or to stand, in the saloon was now a perilous business. Each got to his berth, and kept in it as best he could. Above the dismal creaking and snapping of the cabin woodwork could be heard, now and then, a groan of "Oh my!" from the indisposed. The few ladies on board were sad sufferers; even the old stewardess, whom we discovered with her head down on one of the tables and her arm wound round a post.

The gale increased with the advancing night. To one clinging to the sides of his berth, the mad plunging of the vessel grew, indeed, alarming; occasionally, too, a shock from a sea caused her entire frame to vibrate as if she had struck a reef. No one could keep still enough for sleep, neither in his berth, nor on the floor. Within the state-rooms water-pitchers, wash-bowls, glasses, soap-dishes, life-preservers, and travelling-bags tumbled and bounded about in a truly perilous manner. Everything breakable was soon reduced to a homogeneous mass of *débris*, which flew from one side to the other with each semi-somersault of the ship. Every state-room had its own horrible discord of noises, and these were supplemented by frequent grand crashes in the pantry, where whole piles of plates and stands of glasses broke loose at once. With such sounds, added to the roar of the tempest, the ponderous dashing of the sea, the cracking of the ship, and the ominous "flutter" of her screws as they "raced" in the air when the waves threw them out of water, the night was filled.

SEA-EAGLES FIGHTING.

Clinging for dear life to posts and door-handles, we made calls of condolence on each other, but many were the bruises received. Moses was much "under the weather," and only entreated to be left alone where he lay, half buried in coats and broken crockery, on the floor of his room. "But what if we have to take to the boats?" Karzy said to him. "What if the ship were to sink?" "Let her go," muttered Moses.

About four o'clock a rumor spread that a part of the cargo in the hold, consisting of large sections of drain-pipe for Vera Cruz, had shifted and was plunging from side to side. This story for a time produced something of a panic, for the vessel listed a good deal. It proved to be an exaggerated alarm, however; on the whole, the old steamer was behaving well, and her officers, though anxious, were calm and fairly confident that she would weather it.

Day dawning soon after, we all felt less solicitous. There is something reassuring in morning light, even though, as in our case, it revealed a wild sky and a grand, almost terifically stormy ocean. Some of the waves were, indeed, enormous; and with every plunge of the ship a wall of water seemed to rise at her bowsprit, and fall from ten to twenty feet in depth upon her bows and forward deck. Then as she rose nobly again to climb the next " mountain " the ball on her flagstaff at the stern would descend level with the billows in her wake.

With a liberal use of lines we made good our position on deck, and enjoyed — such of us as were not too sick — some remarkably grand ocean scenery.

The steward and his waiters essayed to get breakfast, and also dinner, in due course, and ludicrous enough were some of the *tableaux* which here and there a lone effort to take coffee or steak furnished, particularly the erratic efforts of three waiters to capture a large ball of butter, which, despite them all, succeeded in making six flying trips across the saloon.

Still the " norther " blew; but the second night seemed not so bad as the first, — perhaps because we had grown a little used to it, and all the loose crockery was already broken. Moses, too, was better, having, as he stated it, thrown up everything except his patronymic, and had hard work several times to keep hold of that.

On the second morning there was sensibly less wind, though the sea seemed as rough as ever.

" How long may we reasonably expect this thing to last? " Stein inquired of Captain Rettig at breakfast, or our attempt at the same.

VERA CRUZ.

"Well, the longest 'norther' I ever knew lasted but *twenty-one* days," was the encouraging response of that veteran sailor.

These long "northers," indeed, which sweep down through Texas from far up in the wintry heart of the North American continent, are the bane of navigation in the Gulf.

But this proved not to be one of the long ones. On the third morning we waked to find that the wind had lulled. By ten o'clock the sun came out and the sky soon cleared. The lofty white peak of Orizaba was then espied far down in the southwest. By three o'clock the steamer had run in under lee of the sheltering island of Sacrificios, and an hour later took up her pilot and steamed into her anchorage beneath the old fortress of San Juan de Ulloa. We then saw that several vessels had gone ashore in the roadstead, and so rough was the water in the port that it was not till the next day that either the mails or the passengers could be landed.

It seemed good, indeed, to stand on the firm bosom of Mother Earth once more, though the "motion" still lingered in our *head* or *legs*, and it was at least forty-eight hours ere any one of us could fairly walk "straight."

CHAPTER VIII.

THE HARBOR OF VERA CRUZ. — A FONDA. — OFF FOR THE CITY OF MEXICO. — GRAND SCENERY. — "MUCHO POLVO." — MEXICO AT EIGHT P.M. — "TRES PESO" ROOMS. — COLD WEATHER. — A DISMAL SUPPER. — "POR LA MAÑANA." — A MORNING WALK IN MEXICO. — MOSES IN TROUBLE AGAIN.

SAFE through the "norther," we spent a very pleasant day in Vera Cruz, the sea-port of Mexico, on the wind-swept and sun-burnt sand-dunes of the *tierra caliente*.

Despite its evil reputation for yellow fever and other malignant diseases, we found Vera Cruz a very neat, clean little town — in fact, it looks as if it had been made to order somewhere else, and brought here all in one piece. Its harbor, too, is, or will have to be, a made-to-order job; when complete it will cost about $20,000,000. An American has the contract; the stakes for it are driven out in the windy roadstead.

We crossed over to the old stone castle of San Juan de Ulloa, and thoroughly enjoyed a ramble through its many-storied towers, casemates, and "bomb-proofs." Formerly it was deemed the strongest of Spanish America; now it is used mainly as a state prison.

The balance of the afternoon was spent at the handsome rooms and fine library of the Mercantile Club; and at eight o'clock we went, according to custom here, to take our tickets over-night, and have our baggage weighed for the railway to the City of Mexico.

At four o'clock next morning the waiters at the Veracruzano were hammering at our doors. For, although the train does not leave for the City of Mexico till six, it is a way they have here of giving you two hours to get to the station in. The allowance of time seemed all the more liberal from the fact that they give you no breakfast, not even coffee, before starting out. From our American training, we were but ten minutes dressing, and had consequently an hour and fifty minutes to walk to the station, a distance of two blocks. It is one of the peculiarities of Vera Cruz that you need not take a carriage to go to any point in it. A good walker can go clean around the city in ten minutes, and have time left over for a little quiet stroll in the desert outside.

VIEW IN TIERRA CALIENTE.

Fortunately, we were able to get coffee at a little *fonda* near the station,— a piece of good luck which aided, perhaps, by the Mexican coffee, stimulated our artist comrade, Karzy, into perpetrating a most atrocious pun, to wit,— that he was *fonder* of that *fonda* than any other *fond her* whom he had ever met. Coming at such an early hour of the day, before breakfast, too, it nearly crushed the whole party. Our fellow-tourist from Indiana, "Moses O.," was but barely able to stagger across the street to the station; the divinity student seemed also much affected.

The line of railway from Vera Cruz up to the City of Mexico is owned by an English company, and all the first-class cars are in compartments, on the English plan, with side-doors. We went down the platform at five minutes before train time to take our places, but the compartment doors were still locked. When asked to unlock them, the porter, guard, and other functionaries stood stolid and unmovable. What the hitch was we could not conjecture; we were very "green." Stein and the divinity student grew hot about it. They went in search of the station agent, but got very little satisfaction from him, I believe.

It was half an hour before the doors were finally opened; the fact was (at least we were subsequently informed so) that the fellows were waiting to be "feed." One even had the impudence to assert that he had *lost his key*, and to simulate a search for it alongside the car. When the truth dawned upon us, Moses rubbed his hands. "Well, well, if this is n't the richest thing yet!" said he. "Modest, are n't they? Why did n't they tell us what they wanted?"

Owing to delay collecting "fees," — at least there was no other visible cause, — the train got out half an hour late, but it was rather fortunate for us; for by this time it had become light, and almost the first object that gladdened our eyes after getting out of the city was the magnificent milk-white cone of Orizaba towering high above everything else, up in the northeast. "Ah! don't she rise gloriously?" Karzy cried out. "Why she's half way up the sky." Orizaba from the coast is, indeed, one of the world's grand sights, — so surprisingly lofty, so stately, and so ethereally pure in tint; a vision of beauty which morning or evening never would bring satiety nor aught save the purest pleasure.

Speaking of this ride from Vera Cruz up to the City of Mexico, Mr. Ober has very aptly described it as "a journey through three zones in one day." And so it is. For the first hundred kilometers across the *tierra caliente*, you journey in the tropics. This heated region is like a vast hot-house, — a wilderness of rank, green verdure. An odor of vanilla fills the air; everywhere are palms and bananas, and the grass huts of the Indians, in groups, or standing out alone in the deep shade, complete the picture of tropic semi-civilized life.

But, meantime, the train has entered the first dark-green range of hills, and steadily winds its way up to higher ground. Here, trees of the temperate zone begin to be seen in forests; the shrubbery is overrun with morning-glories. There are coffee plantations, and the orange grows wild. Cordova is reached, said to be a populous city, but, like all Mexican cities, much out of sight. Crowds of cotton-clad, swarthy people, Indians, come about the cars at the stations, laden with baskets of fruit, — oranges, bananas, *granaditas*, and custard apples, and trays of *tortillas*, smoking hot; and quaint little brown girls in long gowns and black *rebosos* half shading their faces, look up at the car windows and cry out in their soft voices, "*Señor, quiere comprar fruta?*" There are numerous beggars, too, whose low whine, "*Por niña, niña*," or "*Por San José*," — "For Saint Joseph's sake give us a 'clacker,'" — is a less agreeable feature. The government wishes to suppress beggary, and respectfully advises tourists not to give alms.

BEGGAR.

But ere long this zone is left behind, and pine-clad mountains begin to tower on either hand. We are toiling up heavy grades and skirting vast ravines; a powerful double-headed engine, a "Fairlie," has been hooked to the train; it seems to raise us by main strength. Within a distance of forty kilometers we ascend four thousand feet —

to the verge of eternal snow; and still Orizaba, the beautiful, nearer now, rears its white-tourmaline crown, lofty and stately as ever; yet already our morning ride has taken us to an altitude of eight thousand feet above the sea. The scenery as seen by a traveller from the car window grows terrific; and nervous persons are apt to become personally unhappy. The track winds about chasms whose depths grow blue with mists. A single rail holds the car from these depths, and the consequences of a flaw in the steel assume gigantic proportions. Presently a town is seen three thousand feet below, but so close beneath the window that the car might tumble into it, should the flaw suddenly develop itself; but this is not, for the time, a pleasant subject of conversation. Moses was observed to shut his eyes at this point, and Karzy declares that he saw his lips move. It seemed good to enter a tunnel, — a tunnel appeared so much safer. In fact, we ran through nineteen tunnels, if the divinity student counted correctly.

TABLE-LAND OF MEXICO.

At about three in the afternoon, the scene changed rather suddenly. A sensation of "down grade" began to be felt. We had emerged from amidst the colossal scenery of the Cordilleras upon the dry plateau, or great table-land of Mexico. This is the corn and wheat country, but at this season of the year (February) it wears a painfully sere and arid aspect. The scenery is now that of a great plain, with barren, rugged peaks rising out of it at intervals. Numerous pillars of dust, some a thousand feet in height, are seen slowly moving across the extensive plowed tracts. The train, too, running now at a rapid rate, whirled up a perfect "smother" of dust, which entered the car in choking clouds. All our handkerchiefs were speedily converted into respirators, which afforded, however, but slight relief. This is the disagreeable portion of the trip, and following the fresh air and fine scenery of the forenoon it makes the day end rather miserably; for with a dust-hurricane so dense one could scarcely draw breath, we had little enthusiasm left for the tall peak of Malinche, or the great volcanoes Ixtaccihuatl and Popocatepetl, which were announced in sight at sunset. "They will have to wait," said Moses, and wrapping his head in a linen coat he peacefully relapsed into slumber; and, in fact, there was but one man awake in our còmpartment when the train rolled into the fine stone station of the capital at eight o'clock.

"*Mexico!*"

"And here we are," yawned Karzy, rousing up and shivering, for it was cold; the air gave us a peculiarly raw, thin sensation. Mexico is seven thousand five hundred feet above the sea-level, surrounded, too, by snow-clad mountains.

Getting out with our luggage, we found ourselves in the midst of a dense crowd of people wearing tremendous hats, and wrapped up to their noses in what looked to be horse-blankets; they all seemed to be very cold. At length two coaches were secured, and embarking in them, we were driven to the Hotel Iturbide, named after one of Mexico's two emperors of brief tenure. Mexico, indeed, has a bad climate for emperors. Several electric lights cheered up the darkness of the streets, and gave us glimpses of the great green park of the Alameda, as we drove along. Another lighted up the front of the hotel, which we perceived to be a palatial stone structure, adorned with gargoyles and other carvings. But within the great open *patio* had a very cheerless and cold aspect; it had begun to rain, too, and we found the *preprietario* wrapped up to his nose in a muffler. He did not look amiable either. The scribe mustered all his Spanish, and addressed him with, "*Tiene Usted cuartos por cinco?*" (Have you rooms for five?) "*Si,*" said *Usted*, doubtfully, then held up three fingers and added, "*Tres pesos*" (three dollars). *Tres pesos por cinco?*" queried Stein.

"*No, tres pesos por uno.*"

"Well, what of it?" cried Moses, greatly offended at this premature broaching of the terms on the part of our host. "Who asked you the price? Let us see your rooms."

At length we were established in three rooms up what seemed ten or twelve flights of stairs. After a struggle, water was procured; but no soap nor matches could be had in the hotel, and the only light was a single candle. There was no fire in the rooms, and there could be none, for there are neither stoves nor grates in Mexico.

Finally, we got washed, and, having wiped ourselves on the counterpane of a bed, went down to dinner, as we supposed. It then transpired that there was no table in the hotel, and that the *tres pesos* was lodging, merely. A restaurant was pointed out to us; and, sallying forth in the rain, we were at length supplied with soup, tea, and *pan* (bread in flinty billets). We sat and shivered, as we ate, with our overcoats on, then went back to our wretchedly cold, *tres-pesos* rooms, and turned in, — as thoroughly disgusted with Mexico as is possible for a party to be.

However, we felt better and more hopeful in the morning, though Karzy and Stein complained of sleeping cold, and as soon as it was fairly day started out to get breakfast and see the town. It had rained all night; the sky was lowering and black, and the streets were well covered with sticky, black mud. There was, moreover, a horrible odor abroad, which we at first conjectured to be that of the national beverage, *pulque*, but which we learned to be from the city gas, which is manufactured in part from wood. It upset Karzy's stomach completely. "I never can eat a mouthful in this hole," he groaned.

NEW EXPERIENCES.

The street was full of cotton-dressed, barefooted Indians carrying every conceivable sort of burden, some of them running, and almost the first rod out of the hotel we had a collision with a man with a four-story hen-coop on his back, the bottom story full of eggs, and the others alive with chickens and turkeys. The fellow came trotting plump into us, and the stone flags being slippery (I do not think anybody shoved him), down he went, coop and all, and a general crash of eggs and flutter of chickens followed.

The man got up from under the wreck, muttering, and very *yellow;* and his fellows, gathering in a crowd about us, cried out, "*Disgracia!*" and "*Malo! Malo!*" Stein gave him a silver *peso,* which at once caused his face to brighten; and we got away without further disturbance, but had not gone a block when another collision occurred between Moses and two Indians carrying a Mexican gentleman in a chair. "Why, these are the most get-under-foot-people I ever saw," cried Moses. "A man cannot walk here."

But it turned out that we were the get-under-foot party ourselves; we were trying to pass people by turning to the right; in Mexico one must turn to the left, and this is a matter worth attending to when you meet an Indian porter with a load of green beef on his back, approaching at a run.

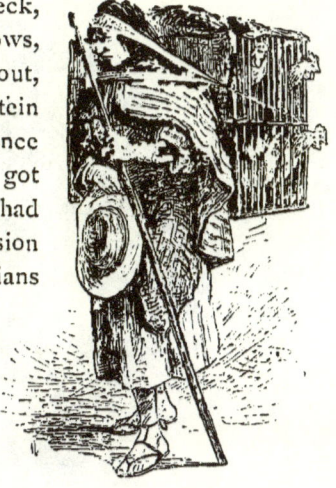

HEN-COOP.

Despite the mud and the lowering sky, our first impressions of the city were rather favorable. Somebody has said that "Mexican houses are all jails" in appearance, being in the Spanish style of architecture, with barred windows and enclosed stone-paved *patios.* In the

City of Mexico the houses and churches are all stone-built, and often very prettily ornamented. The streets are broad, and cross at right-angles. Looking down a street anywhere, you can always see the mountains which wall in the valley. On this first morning of our visit, these were all snow-clad. It was an unusually cold week, we were told, even for winter, the two great volcanoes being commonly the only snow-mountains in sight. We went first to the Alameda, a

CALENDAR-STONE.

pleasant though rather poorly-kept park, looking like an old forest, then to the Plaza, the grand central public square of the city, where are the government palace and the great cathedral of Mexico. This latter is probably on the whole the finest church in the Western hemisphere. This statement may be challenged, being a broad one, but we think so. In the outer wall, near the southwest corner, is set the famous calendar-stone of the Aztecs, which Stein has made the customary effort to interpret. Many other Aztec relics are to be seen in the Museum, which no tourist should neglect to visit.

By this time *nosotros tenemos hambre;* or, in other words, we were hungry. Even Karzy's nose, diverted by the flowers in the parterres about the cathedral from the sour odors in the streets, had ceased to torture him. A fellow-countryman with whom we fell in directed us to a better restaurant, — the Concordia. Resorting thither, we were served with excellent coffee, toast, and beefsteak. But, oh! the butter! — the *mantequilla*. It was simply *manteca* (lard). Karzy tasted it unsuspiciously; then his but half-quieted stomach took alarm afresh. "Oh, for a pound of good, gilt-edged Yankee oleomargarine," he sighed. Even Moses was observed sedulously scraping the stuff off his beefsteak. "What's the matter, Moses?" Stein called across to him.

"Oh, nothing much," he replied. "Only when I eat lard for butter I like to personally know my hog."

Numerous lines of horse-cars, or *tranvias*, lead out along the causeways from the city to all the suburbs and points of interest. Most of these run first, second, and third-class cars. Entering a car marked Santa Anita, we went out to what is termed the old Paseo, near the canal, by which the Indians fetch all kinds of fruits, vegetables, and fodder into the city in canoes and barges. One barge in particular here attracted the attention of our comrade, Moses. It was loaded with what looked to be "round hogs"; and they were the roundest hogs imaginable. Just the heads and bristles had been removed; the carcasses had not been opened apparently, and the legs stuck up stiff as pokers. Now, Moses is a judge of pork, having been reared in a section of the country where fat pigs abound. "By Jove!" quoth he; "Hold on! Only look at those shotes, will you? Why, those are the fattest pigs I ever saw in my days! They look as if their hides would burst! Wonder what breed they can be? I must find out. We want just that kind of hog in Indiana. Never saw such hard,

smart thrust with it, when, presto! there squirted up from the puncture into his very face, and all over his checked ulster, a singular milky liquor! Moses jumped back and spit. The "hog" rapidly collapsed, and the Indians, who had been observing us, came forward, seemingly aggrieved and jabbering about it. Other Indians, not owners, gathered round, and a horse-laugh rose, in which we all

solid-looking pork, never! Excuse me a moment, gentlemen, I wish to look at those pigs closely."

Moses carries a cane with what Karzy calls a "toasting-fork" in it. Some would call it a sword-cane; you can pull out a long, slim rapier attached to the handle, which is supposed to be a weapon of defence. Moses first gave one of the hogs a punch with the ferule of his cane. Then, wishing to test the quality of the pork, I presume, he drew out the "toasting-fork" and gave the carcass a joined, perforce — except Moses. He gave us one reproachful look; then he looked at the hog again, and seemed on the point of collapsing himself. But just at that moment his eye chancing to fall on a public coach which was passing, he made a sudden break, and captured it. Turning at the door, he shied a silver *peso* among the Indians, then disappeared inside. "*Pronto! Pronto!*" we heard him urging the driver; and away they went at a rapid pace.

"He will leave the country!" exclaimed Stein. "Chase him! Catch him!"

We ran after him a little way, then got another coach, and pursued him in that. But he got to the Hotel Iturbide, and had taken refuge in his room when we arrived. The door was locked. It did no good to knock; we could not raise him. "He's paralyzed," Karzy said. Though we went regularly to knock and call him every hour, nothing was heard from him till evening. He had gone to bed.

Thus ended our first day in Mexico.

Those "hogs" were hog-skins full of pulque, — the national lager beer.

CHAPTER IX.

ABOUT THE CITY. — AN EARTHQUAKE. — THE NEW RAILROADS. — NORTHWARD OVER THE CENTRAL. — MEXICAN SCENERY. — THE GRAND TAHOE. — TALK WITH AN ENGINEER. — LASSOING A LOCOMOTIVE. — QUERETARO. — THE LAST HOURS OF MAXIMILIAN. — LA SIERRE DE LAS COMPAÑAS. — SOME INCIDENTS OF THE EXECUTION.

FOR a good view of Mexico City and the famous valley, one should climb the south tower of the cathedral at the Plaza. You go up a little flight of stone steps to the door of the tower, and pull at the end of a rope which hangs invitingly out. Presently the door opens, as if of its own accord, for you will see no one inside it; but far up the winding stone stair you will find an Indian woman waiting your ascent. To her you pay toll, — *un real*, twelve cents.

There are thirty bells in this one tower, three or four of them of enormous proportions. It is advisable to go up at a time when these religious monitors are not addressing themselves to the population.

The view is a fine one. The city with its environment of green groves, and still greener *maguey* plantations, lies at your feet. To the northeast shines the great Lake Tezcoco. East, west, and north rise the strong mountain-walls of the valley; and in the south tower into the clouds the great white guardian volcanoes, Ixtaccihuatl and Popoctapaetl.

POPOCATAPETL.

Another fine view may be had by ascending — as we did — one of the mountains back of the suburban village of Guadaloupe.

Guadaloupe itself is well worth a visit. Many tourists go there to admire the solid silver railing round the altar in the old church, and to taste the *santa agua* (holy water) of the spring in the Chapel of Our Lady of Guadaloupe. The water gushes up copiously from somewhere beneath the chapel. It is very yellow, and tastes a little like soda water; and it is good for anything that chances to ail you. There is a copper pot to drink it from, and a little box to put your money in. You take off your hat when you enter.

Here, according to the faith of the country, Santa Maria, the virgin, has appeared three times. You cannot well doubt it, for the last time she left her image impressed on the coarse *serape* of a poor Indian. We saw the *serape*. She must certainly have come in forcible contact with it; for there is her impress, or image, as plain as day, driven right into the *serape*. And yet some heedless Americans whom we saw had the temerity to make light of it; some persons are constitutionally without faith. The *serape* is framed in gold.

VIRGIN OF GUADALOUPE.

The view from the mountain is very good. Down to the east lies the great lake, said to be five feet higher than the plain on which the city stands. When Cortez and his band of filibusters first invaded the country and entered the Aztec capital the lake, or lakes, came up into the very streets. Much of the business was then done in boats, on canals. Since the Spaniards conquered the Indians and rebuilt the city, the lakes have been greatly reduced, partly by the *gran tahoe*, or drain, and partly by embankments. Probably, too, there is less rain and greater evaporation than formerly, owing to the burning and clearing off of the forests. But the entire plain rests in water. They have only to dig down two or three feet anywhere, when water appears in the hole.

CATHEDRAL, MEXICO.

Last season (1882) there was an earthquake — a pretty serious affair — which shook the city badly, and cracked many houses. An American lady, who was walking in the Alameda at the time, tells us that the earth shook so violently that it was with difficulty that she kept her footing; and that looking down the long promenade, she distinctly saw the ground *rolling toward her in waves*. This phenomenon is accounted for by the presence of so much water in the plain.

The first ten days of our visit were rendered miserable by cold rain in the city and snow on the mountains every day. Four Indians froze to death in the streets one night; it was an unusually severe time. Everybody suffered, for this is a *fireless* country; there is not a grate nor a stove to be had for cash or affection. When we sat down we were compelled to put on great-coats and gloves. Meantime we changed our memorable *tres-pesos* quarters at the Iturbide for three rooms in a house on the Alameda; very comfortable rooms, and fairly well-furnished, for Mexico, at the rate of seventy-five dollars per month. I mention the fact for the purpose of showing the average rate of rents in the capital at the present time. Formerly such rooms could have been hired for thirty or forty dollars. But the new railroads, and the sudden rush of Americans into the country, have set everything "booming." Real estate is held at fabulous prices. The city was full of sharp-looking Americans — "schemers." We met them everywhere, some worthy men, and some — well, it would not afflict us if we were never to meet them again. It is to be feared that the Mexicans will form a none-too-good opinion of us from some of our *paisanas*, who are scouring the country on the lookout for "chances."

On the 8th of March we left the city and went to Queretaro, two hundred and sixty kilometers to the northward by the new line of the Mexican Central railway, which at present writing is running its trains to Lagos, and is being rapidly finished up to Aguas Calientes. Within two years the Boston company building it, hope to connect this southern division of their line with the northern division at present built to Chihuahua. Railway connection with the United States will then be complete. Still another narrow gauge line, the *Nacional*, is surveyed and partially built to Laredo, Texas, by way of Monterey. Then there is a proposed Mexican Southern, in fact, six or eight other proposed lines; so that if all these enterprises prosper Mexico will not long lack railroads. Judging from the appearances along the line of southern division of the Central there will be business enough; its cars were thronged with passengers, particularly the second and third class; long, heavy freight trains were passed on the sidings, and great piles of freight lay about the stations.

Our young people visiting Mexico will surely be disappointed in the looks and general appearance of the country; because travellers and writers have been accustomed to speak of it as a land where all fruits, grasses, and trees grow with tropical luxuriance. Travelling north along the Central we saw no luxuriance whatever, but rather sterile, stony, rust-brown patches of plain amidst equally stony, naked hills and mountains. What wood there is looks to be stunted scrub, worthless for anything save poor fuel. Large tracts are covered with prickly-pear, which here grows to an ugly shrub six or eight feet in height. We were even reduced to the extremity of admiring its yellow blossoms. At rare intervals narrow green belts and plats, like oases in a desert, are passed alongside of lakes and rivers. These are produced by irrigation. Many of the cultivated fields are so coated with small stones that even a New England farmer would give them up in despair. Amidst these you will see Indians plowing with a forked stick — a tree which chances to have the necessary crotch. This is still the plow of Mexico, the plow of three thousand years ago; and for a forked stick it does its work remarkably well; I doubt if an American mould-board plow would work at all amongst the stones.

Still further north the land is not all as bad; there are some fine areas of good soil; but the air of aridity and desolation remains. It is the aspect and scenery of the great Rocky Mountain chain, the general features of which are the same from Patagonia to Alaska. Some states of Mexico, like Michoacan, and some districts along the coast, are different; but it is a mistake to picture Mexico as in any sense a luxuriant country. As compared with the United States east of the Mississippi, it is a sterile and a desolate country.

And the people, the common people, — well, they are Indians, the descendants of the Aztecs and other tribes whom the Spanish subjugated. On these stony tracts they live in little stone huts; on clayey tracts they live in adobe or mud huts, and in the *tierra caliente* they live in grass and palm huts, — always in huts, often in an utterly meagre, dirty condition. What railroads and other modern improvements will do for them remains to be demonstrated.

The country proprietors live at ranchos on their haciendas, or large farms, in more or less comfort; it is rare that one sees a really pretty or picturesque place. Throughout Mexico the hamlets and small cities all look alike. There is the church, or churches, the stiff whitish blocks of stone

A DANGEROUS ADVENTURE.

houses, the "plaza," and the belt of trees; at a distance of a mile it would be difficult to distinguish one from another.

At a distance of forty or fifty kilometers from the City of Mexico, the train entered and ran along the side of a very singular cañon. It looked strangely, as if excavated by human labor, yet seemed far too long, too deep, too vast.

"What can this gorge be?" Karzy exclaimed.

"This? Why this must be the *gran tahoe*," said Stein.

It was, indeed, that stupendous tunnel, or drain, devised and dug by the Conquerors to protect the valley of Mexico against possible inundation. For the lakes of the city valley, having no outlet save from evaporation, were liable to rise on some exceptionally wet season and drown out the city. For three or four miles a niche has been dug along the side of the *tahoe* for the railway. Looking out of the car window, you see the water foaming along the bed of the drain a hundred or a hundred and fifty feet beneath. From earliest time it has been a place fatal to human life. Sixty thousand Indians are said to have lost their lives here when the *tahoe* was dug. Originally the drain was a tunnel, and five thousand perished at a single cave-in of the superincumbent ledges and earth. A car-load of Americans may be the next victims. Our comrade, Stein, has conversed with the engineer of the road, who asserts that the road-bed here rests on *tepicaddy*, and is as "firm as a rock." Engineers ought to understand their business, and generally do; and time may demonstrate the adamantine character of *tepicaddy*.

Journeying on, a diversion was suddenly created by so vigorous an application of the air-brakes, that we were all nearly driven out of our seats. The train came to an abrupt halt. Getting out, it was found that we had run over a Mexican on horseback. The horse was killed, but the man had landed on his feet unhurt. These people will persist, despite all warning, in riding their horses on the line. In this case the fellow was riding toward the train; the track was a straight line, and he must have seen the locomotive two miles away.

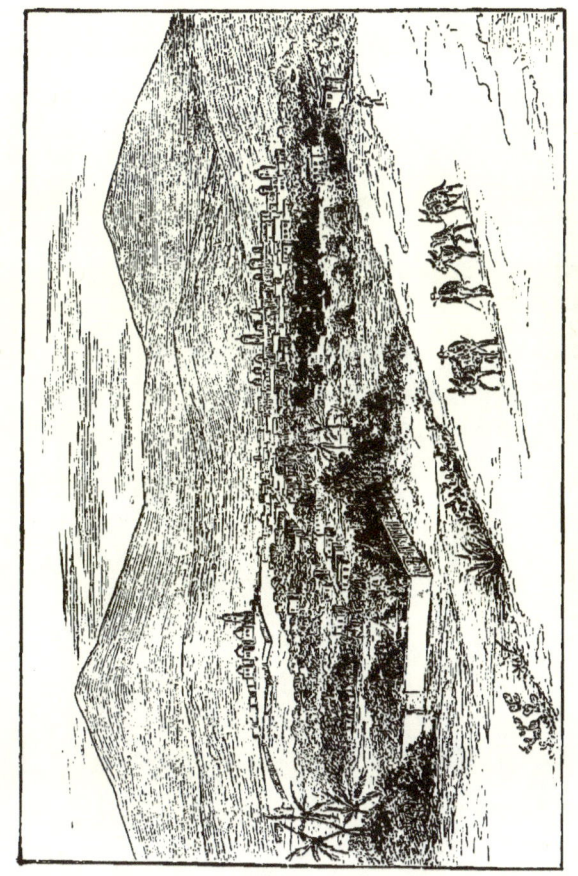

QUERETARO, FROM THE HILL OF BELLS.

"Was he trying to commit suicide, or what?" Moses asked the engineer.

"Suicide! no! he's too big a blessed fool for that!" exclaimed the man of valves and levers, who was greatly disgusted. "He thought he'd have time enough to get off, or he thought I'd stop; or, perhaps, the blessed lunkhead was asleep on his horse."

"Well, he got waked up that time," said Karzy.

"Yes, and he'll go now and try to make the company pay for his horse," said the engineer. "And if I'd happened to kill him they would' have had me in jail six months for it. That's the kind of folks they are here."

Meantime the Mexican stood looking stolidly at his expiring horse, with now and then a sullen glance at the locomotive. Several persons spoke to him, but he made no reply.

"In my mind's eye," said Moses, "I see that chap putting a little pile of stones on the track some dark night."

"Yes, they do that," said the engineer, a Massachusetts man. "They did it a good deal when we first began to run here last season. I'd often see a heap of stones on the rail ahead. At first I used to stop and pick 'em off; I got sick of that and paid no attention to them. The cow-catcher or the wheels will always knock 'em a-going. The blessed rascals are too lazy to put on big ones. When they found I paid no attention, they stopped it."

What this man said about being put in jail, had he chanced to kill the Mexican on horseback, was by no means idle talk. Later in the day we conversed with another engineer who had been in jail two months, I think he said, for killing a "rural" who had tried to lasso the locomotive. These "rurals" are a kind of mounted police for the back country; wild fellows, but pretty good soldiers. This one had probably taken too much pulque. Seeing a train coming, he dashed out from behind some bushes, and flung his lasso at the funnel of the engine. It missed the funnel, but caught on the whistle. The other end of the lasso was tied fast to the saddle as usual; and these lassos are inordinately strong lines of braided green hide. It held, and in an instant Mr. "Rural" and his horse were swung up against the side of the tender with a tremendous thump, which killed both. Wherein the engineer was blamable was not easy to see, yet he was arrested and put in jail, pending a long-winded examination of the affair.

Six miles below Queretaro the line passes through a perfect little paradise of a valley, — a leafy green garden, along a small river with high, rocky, barren mountains on each side. Amidst the trees there is a considerable city, half-hidden; and soon we passed three or four cotton factories. This is the seat of Señor Rubio's attempt to manufacture cottons in Mexico. As yet it is an experiment, but bids fair to be moderately successful. The power for the factories is in part from steam and in part from a very singular and copious spring, which gushes from the mountain-side in volume of about a cubic meter of water per second.

Passing beneath a lofty aqueduct, we were soon at Queretaro, thought by many to be the prettiest city in Mexico. It is situated in the midst of a rather dreary landscape, but is a cleanly, well-built town, with pretty churches and shady plazas. We were very decently lodged here for Mexico, at the new hotel, Ferro-Carril (Railroad House), where we found a jolly landlord, who really exerted himself (a most unusual thing in this country) to make us comfortable.

It was here in Queretaro that the unfortunate Emperor Maximilian made his last stand against the patriot army under Juarez. The town still bears marks of the final bombardment. Deserted by the French, who had placed him on the throne of Mexico by force of arms, the poor fellow had still a great many warm friends, endeared to him personally as well as from hope of political advancement. And in Miramon, Mexia, and Mendez he had three able and devoted officers,— all Mexicans. Mendez was shot as soon as taken, by order of the patriot general. They stood him up against the wall of the square next the railway station, and shot him in the back for a traitor to his country. He resisted to the last, and kept whirling round and crying, "Shoot me in the breast! I am no traitor!"

Miramon and Mexia were imprisoned for some months along with Maximilian in the old convent here, and finally executed with him in 1867.

The people here speak of Maximilian as a good-hearted and kindly man, but weak in character. They say that the patriot leaders did not really wish to shed his blood, and that he might have escaped his hard fate had he been willing to go out of the country privately. Señor Rubio paid seven thousand dollars out of his private purse to a company of soldiers to take him down to the coast, and put him aboard some vessel. Finally, on the night before the execution, everything was "fixed" with the guards and their officers for his escape, and a priest sent to him to acquaint him with the fact. "But what of Miramon and Mexia?" he asked the messenger. "Oh, they will be shot for a certainty," was the reply. "Go back," he said. "I will accept no terms which do not include them."

The truth seems to have been that Maximilian did not at first realize his personal danger, having too much faith, perhaps, in "that divinity that doth hedge about a king," and that finally he acted from an exalted sense of honor.

When he received intelligence that the French army had been ordered home from Mexico, he is said to have stamped on the floor and to have exclaimed, "They leave me no choice betwixt death and disgrace!"

The United States acted well and with dignity in this affair, and its action has done much to heal the breach between the two republics occasioned by the war of 1844. The French invasion of Mexico was an outrage upon both republics. It was made at a time when the United States was powerless to resist it on account of the civil war.

Immediately after that war was finished our government, through Secretary Seward, despatched a note to the French Emperor, giving him in plain terms six months to withdraw his forces from Mexico. The Napoleonic fox did not need a second invitation, and his unfortunate ally, the Austrian Grand Duke, was abandoned to the tender mercies of the Mexicans. As speedily as possible the various French garrisons were withdrawn from the different states and cities, and concentrated at the City of Mexico. From this point they sallied forth one fine morning, with banners flying and drums beating, to march down to the coast at Vera Cruz. The Mexicans stood at their doors and

MAXIMILIAN.

CARLOTTA.

hooted them out of town. During the period of occupation they had ransacked Mexico thoroughly from Tehuantepec to Chihuahua, and taught the Mexicans more tricks than they had learned before in a hundred years. "We were bad enough before they came," the Mexicans naïvely say; "but the French have taught us new deviltries."

Left with "no choice betwixt disgrace and death," Maximilian seems to have deliberately chosen the latter, despite the efforts of his friends and the entreaties of his heroic wife. Mr. Seward is known to have recommended that his life be spared. Juarez replied, "A great and powerful nation like the United States can afford to be merciful; Mexico is too poor and weak."

The place of execution is a dreary little hill, sparsely covered with thorn scrub and prickly-pear, and strewn with rusty-brown stones. They call it the *Sierra de las companias,* the hill of the bells; it is not quite a mile out of Queretaro. The three doomed men were taken from the convent out to this desolate spot in three of the public coaches. A priest accompanied Maximilian. The spectators tell some rather pathetic incidents of the morning. The priest became so affected that he fainted. Taking a little bottle of smelling-salts from his pocket Maximilian kindly assisted to revive him. From some cause the door of his coach stuck fast; he stepped lightly out through the panel, having lowered the glass drop. The entire patriot army was drawn up on and around the hill, and a wall of adobes had been laid up behind where the unfortunate men were to stand to receive the bullets of the firing party. It was arranged that Maximilian should stand in the centre, and the wall had been built a little higher there, he being the tallest of the three. But when they got out, Maximilian said to Miramon, "You shall have the post of honor, general; you shall stand at the centre and I at your left." And half playfully, half lovingly, he placed Miramon in the middle.

The officer in command of the firing party interposed and said, "It cannot be so, señor."

"Surely so trifling a request as this need not be refused," Maximilian said, gently.

One of the Mexican generals, sitting on his horse a few paces away, moved his hand in token of assent, and it was so arranged.

When they had taken their places, Maximilian made a few quiet, unaffected remarks. It was the lot of men of his station in life, he said, to either live for the good of the people or be martyrs; that he had wished well to Mexico, and that he earnestly hoped that his blood would be the last blood shed in civil dissensions.

A few doubloons still remained in his purse. He handed it to the officers, and asked them to distribute them to the soldiers of the firing party — "to the poor fellows who have this last disagreeable duty to perform for me."

He then placed a handkerchief over his beard that it might not be burned by the powder, for the squad had been ordered to stand very close, within six or eight feet. This was his last act before receiving the fatal discharge. All three met their fate bravely and decently,

DEATH OF MAXIMILIAN.

and they suffered badly. The first fire was not fatal, and had to be repeated.

The adobe wall has crumbled away; but pits for three black crosses have been excavated on the spot where they stood. Karzy and Stein brought away each a bit of stone from the pits.

CHAPTER X.

THE OVERLAND PARTY. — THEIR EXPERIENCE WITH THE BRIGANDS. — "PEACE POLICY."

IT may be time to return to the other members of our party, who, it will be remembered, left Chihuahua overland for the City of Mexico at the time of our trip to the former city in the previous November. They proceeded by diligence to Durango, San Luis Potosi, and Aguas Calientes, the present northern terminus of the southern division of the Central railroad.

But they made many detours to various towns in the Cordilleras, on either side of the main route southward. Both Brett and Forney were much interested in the subject of Mexican mines. Wash and Harold, on the other hand, found greater pleasure in looking up the agricultural products of the country.

On the main stage route from Chihuahua southward they were not molested by brigands. The present firm government of Mexico, with its strong corps of "rurals," has well-nigh exterminated those old-time pests of the traveller. There is very little danger now on any of the main roads. Upon some of the more remote routes a "hold-up" is occasionally reported; but the "rurals" are quite certain to ferret out the robbers. When caught the bandits are usually executed on the spot, — a process of justice which, compared with some of the long-winded and uncertain trials of highwaymen in our own West, has its advantages.

On one road only did our four friends have any trouble. This was in the sierras between Cumuripa and Oposura. They had been cautioned in advance at the hotel in the former place; and, as they were to return by the same route, they left all their valuables and took no money with them, save barely enough to defray expenses. Brett had eleven little American gold dollars. These he put in the lining of his boot. Harold put a five-dollar piece upon a corn on his great toe, and did it up with a bit of cotton rag. Forney, not to be beaten, put a five-dollar piece up in his left arm-pit with a piece of court-plaster over it. Wash did not believe they would be molested, and carried his money in his pocket, as usual.

They were the only passengers in the diligence, with the exception of a young Mexican officer named Rivera, who spoke some English, and whom they found a very intelligent and pleasant fellow-traveller.

INDIAN HUT.

According to custom, the diligence left Cumuripa at nine in the evening. Naturally, as they rode out of town, the conversation turned on the chance of a "hold-up" on the road. The young Mexican, Captain Rivera, was inclined to treat the matter very coolly; and in case they were attacked he advised us not to run the risk of resisting, but let the brigands take what they liked. Some of the party were sure to get killed if they tried to beat them off, he said. For the brigands were generally a party of twelve or fifteen, and before stopping

CHURCH AT SANTIAGO.

the diligence they were all stationed, and stood ready to shoot at a signal from their leader, who commonly came forward alone.

His views so far wrought on three of our friends that they took the cartridges from their revolvers, and decided to adopt a peace policy. Forney, on the other hand, declared that he would fill the first brigand who showed his head " with more holes than a pepper-box," and placed his pistol, a large Colt's six-shooter, convenient for carrying out his threat, in his outside coat-pocket.

They journeyed on. There was a bright moon, but it was a tiresome and rather dusty ride, amidst scenery characteristic of the Mexican Cordilleras; rust-brown hills, covered with prickly-pear cactuses, eight and ten feet high, a few straggling mesquite thickets, and at intervals a scanty creek with a fringe of green *souse* brush. Near the creeks were commonly a few Indian huts; otherwise the country was an uninhabited desert.

The dews and the chill at length drove all five of our travellers inside the coach, and as the night drew on they all fell asleep.

From I know not what dreams of silver-mining they were at length suddenly roused by a shout of "Alto!" followed by an abrupt pulling up of the diligence, — so abrupt, in fact, that they were all pitched out of their seats, and left clawing about among the straps and supports. And before they could half regain their seats or take in the situation, a horseman, whose silver-bangled legs shone in the moonlight, pulled open the door of the stage, and in accents which admitted of no delay, but withal very politely, requested them to get out.

"*Dispense me, señors*" (Excuse me, gentlemen), "but you will be so good as to descend."

Good as his word, Forney made a grab for his pistol; but, strange to say, could not find it. First in one pocket, then in the other, he dived his hand. It was gone. Fortunately the darkness inside the diligence prevented the *caballero* at the door from perceiving his motions, else very likely worse would have resulted.

The Mexican officer at once got out. Wash, Brett, Harold, and, finally, Forney followed him, and all stood in a row in the road.

In the semi-darkness they saw eight or ten horsemen sitting in the shadow of some tamarind trees. Four heavily-sombreroed fellows in jackets, with guns, stood on either side of them. Two others came forward. "*Su dinero y reloj, señor*" (Your money and watch, sir), the leader of the gang said to each in turn.

"*No tengo mucho,*" replied Captain Rivera, laughing. "*Tres pesos* (three dollars) *no mas. No tengo un reloj este tiempo.*"

Wash handed over his pocketbook, which, however, contained but eighteen dollars.

Brett alone had taken a watch, — a cheap "Waltham." This he gave up.

But the net result was so unsatisfactory to the brigand leader that he ordered his two aids to search the party. This they did pretty thoroughly, and also searched the diligence, but found nothing of the concealed gold. The pistols they did not seem to care for, or else were too considerate to take.

In no very good humor the robber captain bade them resume their places in the stage; yet he did not fail to give them "*Buenos noches*" and "*Adios*" at parting.

Once inside the diligence, and on their way again — and by this time fully waked up — our friends were much inclined to laugh over the adventure; though Forney wondered greatly what could have become of his revolver. A diligent search on the floor of the coach was made. But the weapon appeared to have "dropped out."

They had proceeded no more than three *leguas*, however, when the diligence was again halted, and they found themselves in the clutches of another band.

It appears that two parties of the robbers had planned to rob the stage that night, — rival bands, it seemed.

A second time our friends alighted to be searched. Captain

Rivera remarked jocosely to the leader that he was behindhand, — that some of his fellows had already plucked the stage. This bit of information seemed to fill the second party with rage and despite. They cursed and swore roundly. For a few moments our friends were in jeopardy, fearing that they would be murdered on the spot. But a few words of judicious banter from the young Mexican officer served to mollify them somewhat.

One of the gang approached Wash, and said, "*Una señora*

YOUNG OCELOTS.

quiere su pannelo, señor" (A lady would like your handkerchief), pointing to a striped silken one which our comrade had tied about his neck.

Wash at once presented it to him.

Another said to Brett, "*A mi me gustan sus zapaterso, señor*" (Your shoes please me).

It was not safe to act reluctant, and our friend saw his eleven gold dollars go along with the shoes.

After this manner our four fellow-countrymen were speedily reduced to shirt, pantaloons, and stockings. Nor did the Mexican officer fare any better at their hands.

The driver of the diligence took no part in the business, either for or against the brigands. Very likely he may have been acting in collusion with them.

The night had been a chilly one at best, and now our travellers had to snuggle close to one another to keep warm.

They arrived at Oposura in a rather forlorn condition, so far as appearance went.

As they were getting down at the hotel, Capitan Rivera quietly drew forth Forney's revolver from under his seat, and presented it to him with many apologies, and sincerely begged his pardon for what seemed a trick.

"I saw, señor," said he, "that you were in earnest about shooting. But it would have been a great mistake, and it might have got us all killed. I am going to turn out the 'rurals,' and instead of those rascally brigands shooting us, I hope to have the great pleasure of having them all shot by to-morrow evening."

Such are some of the phases of life in a back-country State of Mexico.

CHAPTER XI.

BRETT AND FORNEY GO IN QUEST OF COAL MINES, AND HAVE A SINGULAR ADVENTURE WITH A MEXICAN COUNTRY GENTLEMAN.

MAN who can discover a coal mine in Mexico will assuredly make a fortune, the size of which will be limited only by the size and quality of the mine.

More than anything else Mexico needs coal. There are silver mines enough, and, judging from present appearances, there will soon be railways enough. But both silver mines and railroads need coal,— need it imperatively; and thus far no one has discovered coal in quantities or of quality worth digging. The railways are now burning the wood of the mesquite scrub, or pine brought from the higher slopes of the Cordilleras — stripping the country of what scanty forests still remain on its arid and sunburnt surfaces. It seems a pity! Mexico suffers from lack of forests and the moisture which they draw and retain. The entire plateau is parched by drouth. In the time of the Aztec empire, three hundred and seventy years ago, the country was clad with grand old woods, even to the mountain-tops. Irrigation was not then needed; now nothing can be raised without it. The reason of this change is that the Spanish conquerors ignorantly felled and burned off the forests, that their "New Spain" might resemble Old Spain, it is said.

Geologists and mineralogists do not speak encouragingly of the prospects of finding coal measures in Mexico. But these gentlemen have made so many mistakes in their estimates of the mineral wealth of various countries that no one need feel certain that Mexico may not have an ample coal supply safely packed away beneath the strata of some or all of her States.

Two acquaintances of the writer — amateur geologists and mining engineers — have of late been peering about certain portions of the great plateau in the hope of finding indications of the much-needed "black diamonds" of industry; and on one of their prospecting trips in the State of Durango, they had an experience which throws a peculiar light on the character of some of our "neighbors" in the sister republic to southward.

THE HERD OF MOUNTAIN-SHEEP.

At a place up among the mountains, on what from all appearances seemed to be nobody's land, so craggy and well-nigh inaccessible was the locality, they discovered, not coal, but a very promising fissure vein of silver ore, which they determined to "locate," or "denounce," as the phrase is in Mexico, under the very liberal mining law of the country. A mining claim may be made, regardless of any prior ownership of the land by any one; and by the payment of a very small annual fee it remains the property of the discoverer.

SILVER MINE.

For stakes to indicate the bearings and for fuel for their camp-fire that afternoon, they had the two Mexican boys who carried their luggage, etc., fell two small ash trees, which stood in the ravine below their "lead." These were crooked, gnarled little saplings, not more than four or five inches in diameter, of no value; there were a score others just like them along the ravine where they made their camp for the night.

Just at sunset an Indian laborer passed down the ravine carrying a large *jarra* of *zasamoras* (blackberries) on his head. Mr. Forney, one of the two Americans, spoke to him, and asked him to sell some of the zasamoras. The man stood at a distance, and would not reply or come to their fire; after observing them for some moments he went on. His manner gave them some uneasiness, and one or the other of them kept awake to watch lest the fellow might return after dark with a party to rob them. The night passed without incident, however; but as they were taking coffee next morning they saw a large party coming up the ravine, picking their way, on horseback. It was headed by a well-mounted Mexican in short black jacket, silver-trimmed pantaloons, and a richly-ornamented sombrero. Behind him came ten or twelve cotton-clad peons (Indian laborers), all armed with carbines and pistols or knives.

"Well, well," exclaimed Forney, "here comes a whole Mexican army. We are taken, I guess."

Mr. Brett, the other American, stepped forward to meet them, and said in Spanish: "*Buenos dios, señor?*" (What can we do for you?)

Instead of returning the salutation, as most Mexicans will very politely, whatever their errand, the man pointed angrily to the stumps and brush of the two ashes, and began a long, loud tirade which the peons chorused with confirmatory grunts. Our two countrymen knew enough Spanish to understand some portion of what the Mexican was saying; and they readily recognized the words *arboles* (trees), *corta* (cut), and *danos* (damages).

It was plain that their handsomely gotten up and early visitant felt aggrieved, and was demanding damages for the two little ash trees. The two Americans could hardly keep from laughing. Such a cavalcade and such a fuss about so trifling a thing! They were willing enough to pay for the wood.

"*Esta bien*," said Brett, with difficulty retaining a grave face (All right). "*Quanto?*" (How much?)

But their faces lengthened without effort when they heard the man's demand. To their amazement he exclaimed, pompously, "*Dos cientos pesos!*" (two hundred dollars).

They could not believe it. "*Usted quiere doz pesos?*" said Forney (you want two dollars).

"*No Senores, yo quiero dos cientos pesos, y dos cientos pesos yo tomari!*" cried the Mexican, most emphatically; and at the same time he made a sign to his peons, who closed round the two Americans, carbine in hand.

PROSPECTING.

Our two friends hardly knew what turn to give the affair. The demand was outrageous. They had hardly that amount of money by them. To resist by force of arms in that remote spot was out of the question. Not a little disturbed, they attempted to remonstrate with the fellow; but their indignant objections were met by a general cocking of guns on the part of the peons, who evidently waited but a word from their padrone to shoot.

"*Queiren a pagar me?*" (Will you pay me?) was the peremptory question of their captor.

"*No podemos*" (We cannot), Brett replied.

"*Venido conmigo*" (Come along with me, then), was the next equally peremptory requisition. As the only alternative was to fight,— ten to one,— our two friends made a virtue of necessity, and went along as bidden.

They proceeded three miles or more and came out to a rancho upon a haciendo of which their captor was apparently the proprietor. The buildings were surrounded by a high wall or corral of adobes. When they had entered within the enclosure, the Mexican repeated his demand for two hundred dollars. They told him that they could not pay it.

"*Bueno*," was the dogged response. "You will stay with me till you do." Whereupon he ordered them into one of the low stone buildings with barred windows.

The idea of being shut up as prisoners in such a hole was so repugnant to both that they demurred going, and, consulting together, determined to pay the two hundred dollars, and trust to fortune to get out of the country.

They accordingly handed over the money, though they had barely eight dollars left, and were allowed to depart without further plucking. Successful extortion, indeed, put the Mexican in so good a humor that after the customary formula of Spanish politeness, he asked them to come again to visit him, saying *that his house and all*

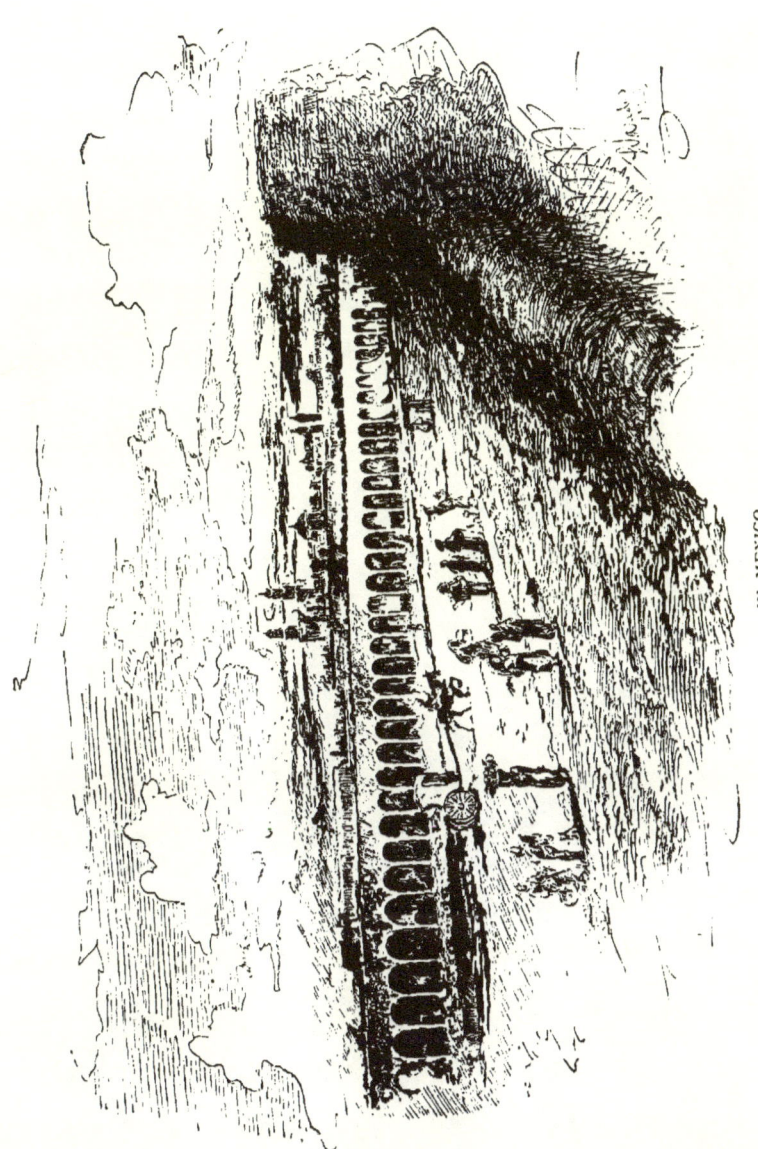
IN MEXICO.

there was in it was theirs. On their part, they would not allow him the satisfaction of observing their chagrin, and very carelessly and good-humoredly bade him good-day and *adios.*

They went back to their camp and looked at their two-hundred-dollar *stakes* — as philosophically as they could. But look at it as they would, they were badly off, — in the midst of a foreign country with no money, or only eight dollars, and two hired Indians on their hands, to whom they already owed twenty dollars. Under such circumstances the reader will, perhaps, excuse Mr. Brett for summing up their financial condition in the one characteristically Western term — "busted;" to which Forney responded, "Busted clean open!"

"What do you say?" Brett questioned. "What's to be done?"

"Can't you ask me an easier one?" said Forney. "But I say," he exclaimed, "it's too bad to let that blessed Mexican get away with all that money."

"True," said Brett. "But how can we work him?"

"Can't say," replied Forney. "But let's go back to his place by-and-by and tell him we want some dinner. He *invited us*, you know, and he cannot well refuse us now that he has got all our money. We will eat with him, talk to him, and draw him out one way and another. We may catch some hold on him."

Accordingly, towards evening, they went back to the rancho, with their two peons, and as politely and nonchalantly as possible asked the proprietor for something to eat. He seemed a little surprised, but welcomed them with grave courtesy, and at once asked them to dine with him.

At dinner our two comrades tried him on various subjects. First, they told him of the mine they had discovered on his estate, and tried to get him in as a partner to work it with them. Then they offered him a contract, which they had the refusal of for ties for the proposed new line of railroad through the State, and many other schemes.

But their host only shrugged his shoulders, in the peculiar style of these people: "*no quiero,*" he did not care for anything of the sort; he had produced a pack of cards, and the peons brought in a roulette-

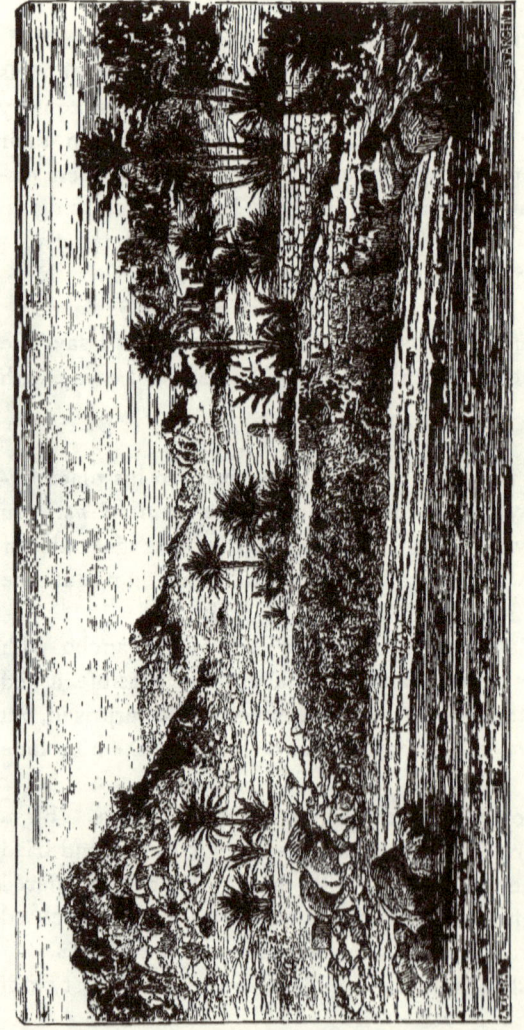

SILVER COUNTRY.

stand and another game of bolas, or balls for guessing and betting. They saw that the only thing likely to interest him was some gambling operation.

Our two friends were not young men of that stamp. They declined to play at three-card monte, or roulette, and were cold on the subject of betting with the bolas. They found, however, that nothing else would interest him, and that, cold on everything else, he was crazy on the subject of gambling, like many others of his nation. Finally they were led into several peculiar wagers with him, in which Yankee shrewdness was curiously matched against Mexican tricks. It may be a fact not known to all readers that every Mexican is named from the saint in the Catholic calendar whose day chances to be his birthday. For example, if a boy is born on the 17th of January, he is named Antonio, that being the day of the saint of that name. So that if you hear a Mexican lad addressed as Antonio you may know at once that his birthday is the 17th of January, and so with all.

Brett had learned this usage since coming to Mexico, incidentally; but Forney knew nothing of it.

As they talked, the Mexican asked them their names, and they showed him their sirnames in their passports — merely pointing them out to him, but not allowing him to see anything else. He then asked whether their ages and the dates of their births were set down in their passports.

They told him they were. He then turned to Forney and said, — " I bet you dollar to dollar (*aposto peso a peso*) that I can guess your birthday.

It came out afterwards through the peons that, in their flurry paying the two hundred dollars, they had unwittingly dropped an old envelope with Forney's name, Gerald S., on it. The Mexican had picked it up, and thinking that christening usage was the same in the United States as in Mexico, and being a sharp rascal, he laid his wager on that.

Forney was staggered; he was sure the Mexican had not seen the date in the passports. But Brett guessed the game, and saw the mistake the fellow had fallen into. He nodded to Forney to take it up. Accordingly Forney said " *cincuenta pesos*," unhesitatingly, and not having the money he took off his watch and laid it on the table. The Mexican glanced at the watch, and opening a drawer, put out fifty dollars beside the watch, in silver.

" *Bueno,*" said he. " You were born on the 30th of September."

Without a word Forney opened his passport, and showed the actual date, — July 13.

The Mexican looked astonished, but seeing that he had lost indisputably, he shoved the silver across very courteously. Being an acute fellow, too, he at once jumped at two conclusions, that custom was not the same in the United States, and that these two Americans probably did not know the Mexican usage. But to be sure he presently asked innocently enough, "*Conoce mi nombre?*"

"No," said Forney, which was quite true; and he gave no indication of understanding the drift of the question. But Brett had heard one of the women in the rancho address the Mexican as *Benito* when they were at the place in the morning. Again he divined the game; and by a quick effort of memory he placed the day from connecting it with the birthday of Juarez, the Mexican statesman. But Forney remained quite in the dark.

Perceiving Forney's unmistakably blank and innocent face the Mexican said, "I lost. *Bueno.* But I bet you four to one (*cuartro a uno*) you cannot guess my birthday."

Again Brett gave the nod, and Forney, after a moment of discreet doubt said: —

"*Hecho*" (Done), and put down the fifty dollars which he had just won.

"*Bueno!*" exclaimed their host, who was beginning to get excited. Not having two hundred in the table drawer, he went to a chest at the other side of the room for the balance. Meantime Brett scribbled *a date* on the table under his hand with his pencil, on which Forney's eye presumably fell; for as soon as the cash was piled, he said quietly, "*Viente y uno de Marzo*" (March 21).

The Mexican jumped from his chair, and made a half movement to seize the silver. "No, *no!*" he shouted. But several of the peons standing around, all vastly interested in the play, had unwittingly cried out, "*Bueno! Si! Si!*" Seeing it was useless to deny it, the baffled gamester sat down. "*Dispense me!*" he said. "*Usted tiene razon.*"

Forney lost no time in pocketing the cash, and they soon took leave — not just liking the uneasy manner in which the eye of their host burned and roved about. By this time it was late in the evening.

"Old fellow, this is the worst job I ever helped put up," exclaimed Brett as soon as they were outside in the dark. "But I declare he drove us to it. Now let's get out of here before we get our throats cut."

Instead of going back to camp, they made a rapid trip to the village of Zurnal that night, travelling eighteen or twenty miles in about seven hours. And thus far they have not thought it best to go back to "denounce" their mine.

CHAPTER XII.

SANTA SEMANA. — STUDYING SPANISH. — "BOILED BONES." — AT EL PASEO DE FLORES. — A WEEK OF FIESTAS. — THE "JUDASES" AND THE "DRY BONES RATTLING." — GRAND EXPLOSION OF JUDASES. — CORRIDA DE TOROS. — A SUNDAY BULL-FIGHT. — NO END OF A NOISE! — MOSES GETS EXCITED. — "BULLY FOR THE WHITE-FACED BULL!"

SANTA SEMANA, or Holy Week, in Mexico will afford a novel experience to most young people from the United States who visit Mexico during the few years following the opening of the new railways. It is the gayest, the most showy, and by all odds the most spirited season of the whole year, carnival not excepted. Crowds of the Indian people from the surrounding country flock into the city; it is the time of floral decorations, booths, traffic, and pulque-drinking. Now, too, the Mexican ladies come forth in their new dresses for the year — dresses as rich, and even more positive in color than those put on by their fashionable sisters in New York or Paris; and altogether one may gain a better idea of Mexico and Mexicans on this than any other occasion.

On the 13th of March our party (reinforced by the four young gentlemen who had come overland from El Paso and Chihuahua) returned to the capital from our trip to Lagos, Queretaro, and Guadalajara, and established ourselves for the time at our rooms on the Alameda, settled down to see the sights, and study Spanish.

In this latter pursuit, however, several of us, particularly Moses, are having not a little difficulty. That long list of irregular Spanish verbs is a true linguistic "staggerer." Moses, too, who is a very *literal* fellow, finds himself much confounded by words of familiar sounds which have unfamiliar meanings.

"Well, this is a queer country!" he exclaimed a few mornings ago. "Here they call corn *mice* (*maiz*), and call a loaf of bread a *pan;* a trunk they call a *bowl*, and a jug a *harrow* (*jarra*), and country is *pies*. Why, by the time a fellow had learned two or three such languages he would never be sure what he was talking about."

STREET SCENE IN MEXICO.

But Karzy had the "worst thing" a few days since, at the restaurant where we take our meals. He got the words *huevos* which means eggs, and *huesos*, which means bones, mixed in his mind. When the Mexican waiter came to take his order, he said, "*Quiero huesos pasados en agua caliente, cinco minutos!*" (Boiled bones, five minutes.)

"*Que?*" questioned the waiter, deprecatorily.

"*Huesos, cinco minutos?*" repeated Karzy, peremptorily. "*Ven, ven, pronto!*" (Come, be quick!) (At this juncture Stein trod on Moses' toe under the table and sent an obscure wink round, whereat all the others perused the bill of fare with grave attention.)

The waiter started off hesitatingly, went a few steps, then turned as if to come back for further conversation, but seeing a look of wrath mounting in Karzy's face, he thought better of it, and marched off determinedly toward the kitchen.

Meantime the rest of us gave our orders, and waited for the result.

Karzy had to wait some time. At length in marched the waiter, bringing a large platter of beef bones, — two thigh-bones sawn in two and cracked! This appetizing dish he set down steaming hot before our junior comrade, whose face would at once have furnished a good study for Nast. Surprise and indignation are no words for it. He jumped up and glared at the waiter, who stepped back a little, but said stoutly, "*Huesos, señor.*" A snort from Moses drew Karzy's attention to us. Then a sickly smile broke out on his face; he shook his head, took his new sombrero and left without a word.

The waiter collected *dos reales* (twenty-five cents) of us for the *bones*.

We saw no more of Karzy till afternoon.

The old church of San Agostin, a very large one, has been handsomely remodeled in stone to contain the *Biblioteca Nacional* — (National Public Library). There are a few English works, and an immense number of Spanish books and manuscripts. We asked the attendant who showed us through it how many volumes they had, and he put down on a slip of paper the figures one hundred and twenty millions! We presumed that he had added the last three ciphers by mistake, but did not quite like to question his arithmetic. This *biblioteca* really looks to be larger than any public or university library in the United States. Any person can consult the books in the reading-room; but as yet books are not allowed to be taken away on the card system.

There is another public library, called the Cinco de Mayo, less extensive; and three or four others connected with the National Schools of Medicine, Law, and Technology. The city does not lack for books, but rather for people who read; and this is a lack which cannot be supplied till their new public school system has had a quarter of a century to make the children into readers. An admirable new public school system has been organized within the last few years; but its founders will need to have patience to see it make its way slowly amidst the ignorance and idle superstitions in which the Catholic church is more than content to have the people remain. The

A NATIVE LADY.

gigantic influence of the church over the people is now, more than any other cause, what holds Mexico at a standstill. As yet it is only a little shaken; but to that little is due everything which has been effected in the way of national progress. We do not say this in the spirit of scientific radicalism, but merely record it as an easily apparent fact to the eye of any intelligent observer.

But *Santa Semana!* While visiting the various points of interest in the city, its suburbs, and the outlying towns of the magnificent valley,—Chapultepec, Tacubaya, Atzcapotzalco, Guadaloupe, Tezcuco,—we have been enjoying in due course the successive *fiestas* and "exercises" of Holy Week. Not the least pleasurable of these was the *Fiesta de las Flores*, or Flower Festival, of the previous Friday (March 16), at the old Paseo along the canal at Santa Anita. On this day the Indians bring in flowers from their *chinampas* and other gardens, to sell and to decorate the churches. At an early hour the canal for half a league was well-nigh impassable from the throng of their canoes and barges. And flowers, flowers, such quantities of flowers,—queen-roses, roses of Castile, pinks, sweet peas, nasturtiums, poppies, crowns and mounds of poppies of most dazzling hues, pansies, heliotrope, and all the thousand geraniums,—

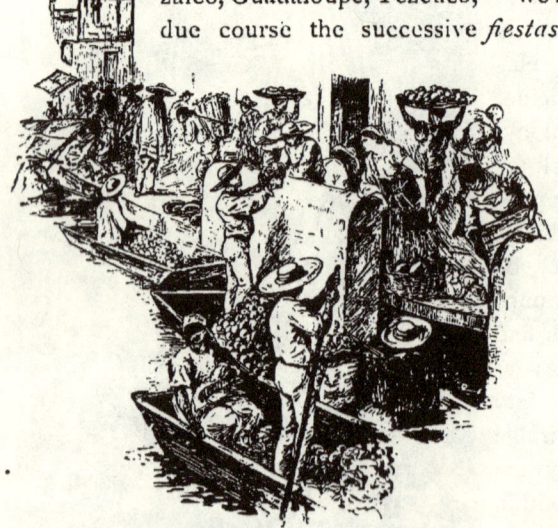

CANAL OF LA VIGA, CITY OF MEXICO.

a perfectly bewildering maze of color and perfume! And all delightfully cheap in price, — so cheap that one would need to have taken a coach, or a horse-car, to get away the heaps he could buy for a peso.

The historians of the Conquest speak of the love of the Indians, at that date, for flowers and flower festivals. They seem not to have changed in taste; and it is along this old Paseo that this gentle, kindly people may be seen and studied at best advantage. We went home from this flower festival with the feeling that never in all our lives had we seen and smelled so many flowers.

Monday following (March 19) was San José's day. All the Mexicans named José, whose birthday was the nineteenth, were on a *fiesta* that day; and, judging from the hilarious crowd, about half the population must be Josés.

As the week advanced the interest in the *fiestas* and the crowds deepened and thickened, particularly at the *zocalo* and about the cathedral. All the events of Passion Week, the arrest, trial, and resurrection of Christ, are at this time simulated in the church ceremonial. The services were continuous.

SCENE DURING SANTA SEMANA.

On Thursday the people in their finest clothing, many of the ladies superbly attired, were constantly going on foot from church to church.

Friday was the day of grief and solemn mourning. No business, save of extreme necessity, was done. The shops were closed; the horses and mules remained in their stables.

Meantime the "dry bones" of Scripture were rattling; every boy had some sort of cart or "jig," that revolved with a furiously snapping spring. There was a racket only equalled by that in a North American town on a Fourth of July morning, when all the crackers and guns are going off. In the Plaza were hundreds of venders, selling "Judases" and "heretics," many of them life-size, and of all degrees of hideousness, to be hung, burned, and blown to pieces at nine o'clock Saturday morning.

And when Saturday morning dawned, and nine o'clock struck, Fourth of July was nowhere! In all the cross-streets and alleys thousands of Judases and heretics, hung on ropes and wires, in all manner of excruciating attitudes, and charged with gunpowder, were touched off, and the city was soon blue with smoke.

At ten o'clock Saturday the bells, all the thousands of church-bells, which for two days had been silent, burst forth in one tremendous, triumphant peal. The mourning was over, the grief had passed. And all the Judases and heretics being by this time disposed of in a satisfactory manner, the multitude went for their next arch enemy, — pulque.

"Big bull-fight at Toluca to-morrow!" exclaimed Karzy, coming

SPANISH BEGGAR IN MEXICO.

in from a stroll to the Zocalo, the second week after our arrival in Mexico. "Railway fare, three dollars; admission to the Plaza del Toros, *un peso* on the shady side; *medio peso* on the sunny side. Say, fellows, shall we go?"

"But to-morrow is Sunday," said Moses.

"*Si, señor;* but they never have a bull-fight on any other day here, — *nunca. Todos Domingos,* — Sunday or nothing."

"I don't believe it will amount to much," Stein observed. "They are mostly disgraceful affairs, I am told."

"But this is advertised for a big affair," urged Karzy. "They have five bulls, — howlers, bellowers, tearers, — and a matador who is a first-class artist in bull-sticking."

"What say, Harold? what say, Wash?" queried Stein. "You've seen a bull-fight in Spain. Is it worth our while?"

"Well, I do not much fancy a bull-fight, myself," replied Burleigh. "Still it is a thing to see — once."

We went.

SPANISH GRANDEE ON HIS WAY TO THE FIGHT.

There is some wonderfully fine scenery along the line of railroad from Mexico to Toluca; some of it is as good as any of that from Vera Cruz up to the city. This alone amply repaid us for the trip. The train arrived at about half-past three in the afternoon; and we proceeded immediately to the Plaza del Toros, and bought seats on the shady side of the arena, — a needless piece of extravagance, for it soon began to rain. There were, for a guess, fifteen hundred people present, mostly typical Mexicans, wrapped up in *serapes*.

Two *picadors*, on rather sorry nags, with their eyes carefully blindfolded, were already in the arena; also three or four gayly-dressed *matadors*, and some other light infantry of the bull-fighting army in Mexico.

We had barely got our seats when the gate of the bull-pen was thrown open, and there rushed out into the ring, evidently impelled by some unseen bradding from behind, a rather indifferent red and white bull of the native breed. He smelled the ground, snorted, and was manifestly scared. Jeers greeted him. The picadors, or "prickers," set upon him with their lances, riding past on their blindfolded horses; and the matadors threw bandarillos (little darts) betasselled with fluttering gilt papers and snapping with powder-crackers, which stuck in the poor, bewildered brute's shoulders and flanks. These were designed to infuriate him and work his courage up to fighting pitch; but they had merely the effect to increase his terror. Immediately he bolted and went round the ring, intent only on escape, with his tail straight in the air. I never saw a bull run better. The matador-in-chief could neither catch him nor head him — to give him the fatal thrust. The picadors made two attempts to lasso him, but he went clear of both nooses.

The crowd roared and yelled and hissed and whistled. There was a most outrageous noise — for Sunday.

At length they lassoed him round his erect and terrified tail, and flung him down in the dirt. The chief matador ran up, and while the bull was struggling to regain his feet thrust a long rapier into his chest. This brave deed done, he held up the ensanguined weapon to the gaze of the audience. But the rabble only roared the louder; and as for the bull, he lay and kicked till hauled out of the arena.

"I'm going home," said Moses.

"Sit still," said Stein. "We're in for it."

A trumpet sounded, and another bull was spurred into the ring. This was a brindled bull; he looked vicious, and began to paw up the sand, but chancing to smell the blood of his predecessor on the ground, he, too, took fright, and with a hideous bawl turned to get back into the bull-pen. Finding the gate closed, and alarmed still more by the shouts and lancing of the picadors, he bolted in turn, and raised a still *taller* tail than the first; but he did not run as well. They soon lassoed him, when he shared the ignominious fate of his fellow-coward.

By this time the crowd was beginning to get wrathy, and to intimate in loud terms that the whole show was a fraud.

But the trumpet immediately sounded again, and a third bull walked in — a tremendously large, calm, good-natured looking fellow, with a white face and grizzled white and deep red sides. His horns were short, but large round; he was a portly fellow. The rabble stopped jeering to look at him.

Meantime the picadors had set upon him with their lances and bandarillos, switching red and orange scarfs in his face, and offering him all sorts of indignities.

They got him roused up at length, and he rushed at the picadors with the roar of a lion! Quick as a flash one horse was tossed up like a sack of bran, and falling partly on the other, both went to the earth in a heap. The picadors, agile as cats, came down on their feet and scud. The first horse lay groaning, fatally gored; the other scrambled up, but being blindfolded, rushed plump on the bull, which threw it at least seven feet clear of the ground at one vengeful toss. The horse fell heavily, and lay quivering, evidently with its legs broken.

By this time both picadors and matadors were pricking and flaunting their scarfs at the bull again. But the beast was "game." He scattered them like chaff; right and left he dived at them, and, for a creature of his size, he turned wonderfully short corners, — uttering never a sound, save now and then a brusque snort.

The crowd cheered, "*Bravo toro! bravo toro!*" And our comrade Moses, too, was getting fearfully wrought up — on the bull's side.

At length the chief matador advanced upon the bull alone, sword in hand. For an instant they confronted each other; then like an avalanche the bull plunged at him with head lowered. The matador was certainly a fellow of nerve; he tossed his scarf across the bull's forehead, and at the same instant vaulting over the left horn of his antagonist, plunged his sword deep into the massive neck, just forward of the shoulder. But he failed to strike a vital part, and the bull turning with one of his gruff snorts, pursued him like a thunderbolt across the arena. The man had no time even to tack; he sprang for the palisade, — to bound over it, — and the horns of the bull just touching him as he jumped, he came over flying, and alighted with a crash on the lower benches.

THE MATADOR.

The audience fairly screamed their applause; and Moses, jumping up on his seat, swung his hat and shouted.

There was a lull for a few moments, while the chief matador picked himself up and got breath. He then entered the arena again alone, with his red *serape* and sword, which he succeeded in plunging a second time into the animal's neck. But next instant he had to jump the palisade again, and had a narrow escape, indeed; the bull's horns were driven into the planks at his very back, with a force which made the whole structure shake. Again the plaza roared with "*Bravo toro!*"

The entire squad of matadors and picadors now entered the arena together; but the bull seeming to recognize at once the chief matador as his worst and most deadly enemy, dashed at him, and regardless of the lances and bandarillos of the others, chased him to and fro, and at length a third time drove him over the palisade.

But all this time the bull had been bleeding badly. It soon became plain that he was weakening.

At length he moved unsteadily toward the further side of the arena, and there turned his back upon his tormentors, not in fear, but as if indifferent now. His blood was flowing fast, and his eyes were fixed on the red pool as if in despair. Yet on the matador's approach to give him a finishing stroke, he seemed to rally his ebbing strength for a moment. His tail lashed his side; and wheeling half round, he plunged heavily at his murderer, but fell headlong from the effort, and with a deep breath gave up his life.

It was really a painful scene.

Meantime it began to rain harder than ever, and not caring to see more we left the plaza, and went to the station.

"This whole business is a relic of barbarism," Stein remarked, as we went along; and so far as our party was concerned, there was no dissent from this opinion.

CHAPTER XIII.

ANOTHER SYNOD. — ITEMS OF INTEREST NOTED DOWN BY DIFFERENT MEMBERS OF THE PARTY, AND CONTRIBUTED BY THEM TO THE GENERAL NARRATIVE.

THE MEXICAN WEST POINT.

BY GERALD S. FORNEY.

THE old palace and fortress of Chapultepec, situated on an abrupt rocky hill four or five miles out of the City of Mexico, is at present being handsomely rebuilt and enlarged for the new Military School of Mexico. Here the cadets of this republic will in future receive their military education. The location differs greatly from that of our own West Point Academy. It fronts on no noble river like the Hudson, and is surrounded by no such rugged scenery; yet the views from the castle-towers are, perhaps, surpassed by none in the world. To the southward lies the great white city, with its hundred domes and towers, as fair now as when Cortes and his fellows first gazed on it, relieved against the broad lake; as fair and as fine as when, three hundred and fifty years ago, it first amazed the eyes of Cortes and his fellow-invaders. North, east, and west the wide green valley, with its long aqueducts and tree-bordered causeways, its *maguey* plantations, and wide expanses of grain, extends off to the high mountain-rim rising to the snow-line, while in the southwest loom the grand snow-clad *volcans*.

The hill of Chapultepec itself rises alone, solitary in this charming landscape; a rusty-brown volcanic pustule thrust up out of the plain ages ago by the fever of the still raging fires beneath the plain. But its nakedness is now beautified by noble ash trees and fine old cypresses, whose tops almost hide the castle-walls on the summit. The hill seems the natural sentry-box of the valley and the city. Within the old portion of the castle at the summit there is a beau-

CHAPULTEPEC.

tiful open *patio* and gardens, upon which the rooms and saloons open. Here Maximilian and Carlotta did a little of their imperial houskeeping, and are said to have spent some happy weeks before the worse troubled times came to them.

In 1846 Chapultepec was relied on by the Mexicans as the guardian fort of the city. It was termed the Mexican Gibraltar. During the American invasion, our troops captured it after a sharp assault and hand to-hand fight. How they ever got up the rocky sides of the hill in the face of a hostile fire, seems a wonderful exploit at arms.

A very handsome monument at the foot of the winding way has been raised in memory of the Mexican officers who fell *en la Invasion Norte Americana,* as the inscription runs, which one of our party freely translated : —

" In the naughty American Invasion," — not without a grain of truth, I fear.

The present Mexican army numbers rather over thirty thousand men. They seem a fairly well-equipped and hardy body of soldiers. It is quite possible that the next nation which attacks Mexico, thinking to find the business a mere holiday excursion, may be a good deal disappointed in the result.

CASTLE OF CHAPULTEPEC.

MEXICAN PAPER.

BY WASH.

ONE of the amusing things in a Mexican shop is to see the aggrieved expression which will come over the face of the shopman, if asked to wrap up the purchases that you have just made of him. And if he attempts to oblige you in

PYRAMID OF CHOLULA.

this respect, you will smile again at the coarse quality of the paper and the stingy little bit which he spares you off the carefully kept parcel under the counter.

But there is good reason for such parsimony. If he were to allow you a large piece, such as an American shopman would use, his profits would disappear with the paper.

Paper of all kinds is very dear in Mexico, though no country is more abundantly supplied by nature with paper-making materials. At present there are few paper-mills in the country, and these small. The demand for paper is rapidly on the increase, particularly printing-paper ; and the tariff on imported papers is high, and likely to remain so. On the various grades of imported papers, including cigarette-paper, the custom-house charges are from ten to seventy cents per kilogramme (2 1-5 lbs.).

The present prices of paper in Mexico, are about as follows : —

Coarse wrapping-paper, from ten to twelve cents per pound. White paper for printing newspapers, etc., from twenty-five to thirty cents per pound. Very ordinary letter-paper, at retail, fifty cents per quire. Common, rather thin note-paper, twenty-five cents per quire.

Here should be a good field for American capital and industry. A score of paper-mills, each in the vicinity of some large town, ought, every one of them, to yield its owner a fortune if rightly managed.

The materials for paper-making in Mexico are abundant and cheaply obtained. The American aloe, *agave*, or *maguey* plant (from the juice of which pulque is made), grows to gigantic size here ; and its leaves yield an immense quantity of tough fibre, which is readily bleached and ground for paper. Four or five kinds of plantain, which grow very luxuriantly in the warm districts, afford a very fine white fibre, in unlimited quantities. A rush, called *tule*, which the Indians now use chiefly for mats, carpets, baskets, and chairs, and which grows plentifully without cultivation, is pronounced a superb paper stuff. The *alacle* and other plants of the *malvaceæ* family grow commonly, especially in the State of Morelos. Many others, the *pochote*, the *cuanlahuac*, the *huinare*, the "pastles," or *henos*, are used for paper, and said to afford the best of material. Then there are numerous plants of the cotton family and *cacti* growing wild, and covering vast tracts of country, all of which are readily utilized for paper-making.

THE MEXICAN EAR-BEAN.

BY HAROLD.

Recently, while out duck-shooting on the shore of one of those incomparable lakes which render Michoacan the most picturesque of Mexican States, the attention of the writer was drawn to a group of native women and children in the woods hard by, busily engaged picking up in baskets what might at first sight have been mistaken for nuts. Curious to know what sort of nuts they were, I drew near and asked a bright little Indian boy what he had there. "*Que tiene en su canistra?*" I said to him.

"*Cascalotes, señor,*" was his instant reply.

"*Y que son cascalotes?*" I queried.

This latter question proved rather a difficult one for the little fellow; but a little girl, a year or two older, and possibly his sister, came forward.

"*Cascalotes son frigoles, señor,*" she said; and I further learned from her that these *frigoles* (beans) were sold by the Indians for a *claco por libra*, — a cent and a half per pound, — and that they went in a great *baque* (ship) across the sea to *Francia* (France), where they were used for tanning *becerro* (leather) for *zapatos* (shoes).

All this from a little tawny Indian girl not more than eleven years old. Furthermore, I learned that this bean was named from its resemblance to the human ear, which surely enough it did look like somewhat; and that in their language it was simply the *ear-bean*.

It was news to me that there was a kind of bean which contained the astringent principle *necessary* to tan leather. I bethought myself of the ruthless manner in which whole forests of oak and hemlock are annually felled and stripped of their bark in the United States and in Canada to procure the material for tanning; and that, too, in sections where drouth from the destruction of the forests is becoming more oppressive every year. It seemed to me that this ear-bean might be imported to stay, in some degree at least, this great evil. I spent an entire day collecting facts concerning it, which may be condensed in the following paragraph: —

These ear-beans grow wild on a small tree, which reaches the height of twenty and thirty feet, with wide, branching limbs. As many as ten bushels of the odd, crooked beans often grow on a single tree. When ripe they fall to the ground, and cover many extensive tracts. Not only in Michoacan, but in Colima and Guerrero, untold thousands of bushels rot ungathered in the forests. It is not difficult to hire the Indians to pick them up at one cent per pound. The little Indian girl told me that she gathered "*dos cientos libras,*" two hundred pounds, in a day. To be used for tanning the beans have only to be dried and ground; and so rich are they in the astringent qualities that a very small quantity of the bean-meal is sufficient to tan a hide. The French tanners, I am informed, have been quite willing to pay ten cents a pound for the dry beans; it is probable that they could be furnished to American tanners for one-half that sum.

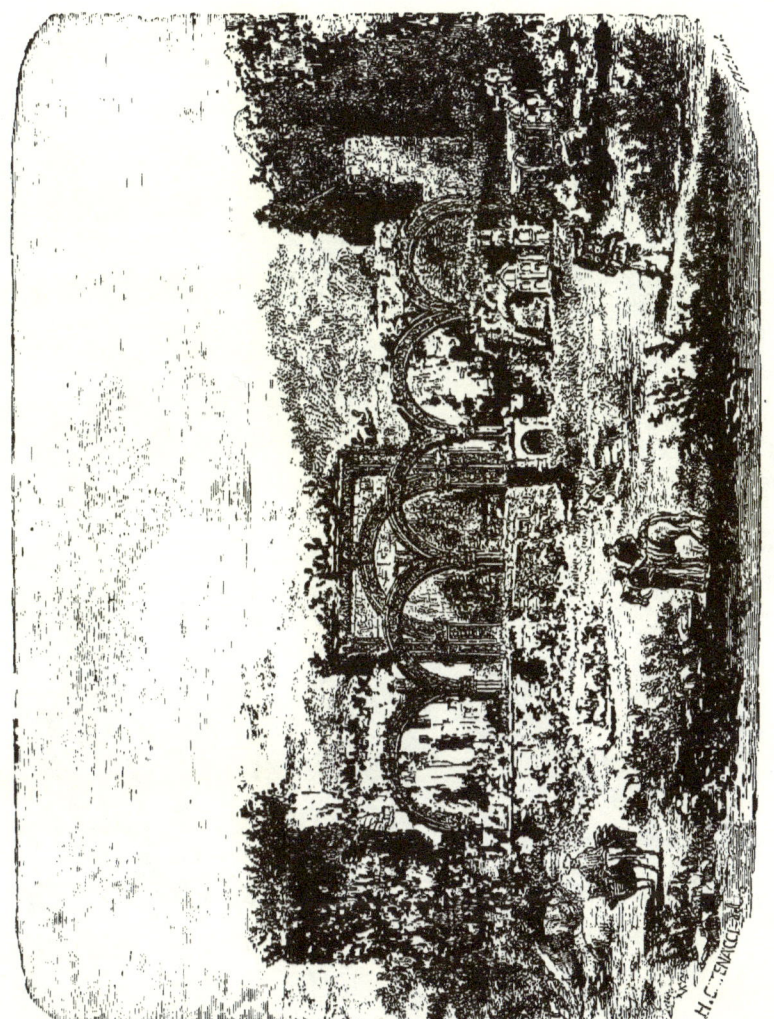

RUINS IN MEXICO.

SOME AZTEC JAWBREAKERS.

BY KARZY.

For fifteen or twenty years past our newspapers and other periodicals have been in the habit of astonishing their readers at regular intervals with a list of the traffic, and apparently unpronounceable names of the Maine Lakes — as a curiosity. For example: Mooselukmaguntic, Apmoogeenagamook, Abolgecarmaguscook, *et als.*

But this list will probably never appear in print again. We take some credit to ourselves for having imported recently from Mexico, at some expense and pain to the printers, another and far superior list, the merits of which we feel sure all our contemporaries will at once recognize. We have not been so selfish as to copyright it. It shall be common property.

Not to paralyze the public we open the list with an easy one — the name of one of the beautiful snow-clad *volcans*, which tower on the southern rim of the valley of Mexico, — *Ixtaccihuatl*. At present it is one of the American tourists' first task, on visiting the Mexican capital, to properly pronounce this word; and it commonly takes him from two days to a week, according to the supple-

MEXICAN WAR-GOD, HUITZILOPOCHTLI.

ness of his lingual apparatus. It should be enunciated, *cats-starts*-sec-*wart-l*, with the accent on the next to the final syllable.

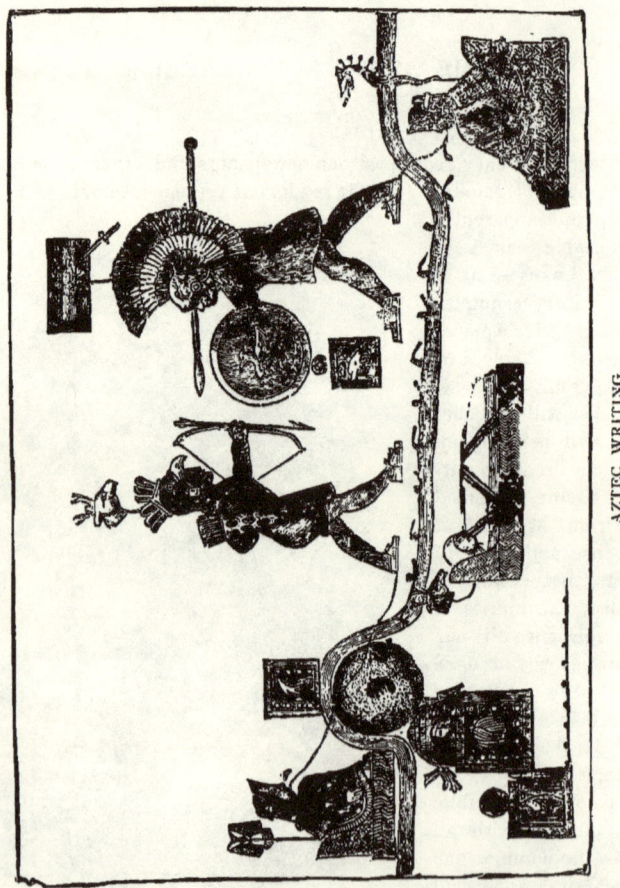

AZTEC WRITING.

Try next the Aztec word for a kiss; we find this with us briefly-named token of affection, much prolonged, — drawn out, in fact. It is *teteuñamiquiliztli*. One can all but hear the shrill smack with which it terminates. It would be a

useless and vain torture of the English alphabet to attempt to depict its pronunciation. This reminds us that the Aztec word for torture is *tetlayhiduiltiliztli*. When this has been decently endured, take, — *Ichpopochtin*, meaning girls; *Telpopochtin*, boys.
Amatlacuilolitguitcatiaxtlahuilli, the pay of a courier.
Tetlatolaniliztli, a demand.
Mimmiztin, cats; and then enunciate softly and distinctly, — *Notlaxomahuiztespixcatatzin*, the Aztec word for their paternal priest.

There are plenty more, but the above will probably suffice for the reader's first exercise in Aztec.

The idols are about as ugly as their names, and bear strange resemblamce to birds, beasts, and fishes, as well as to humanity.

The open mouth of a beast often discloses a human face, as in the accompanying illustration.

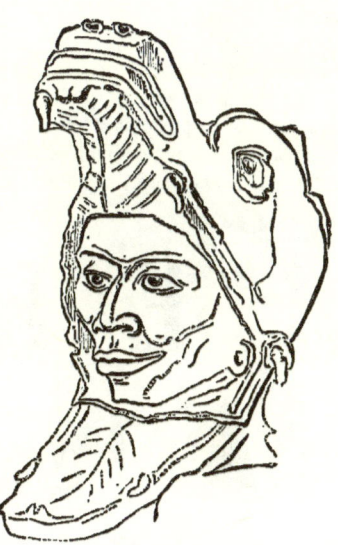

AZTEC IDOL.

It is remarkable what a number of archæological treasures are being continually unearthed, which are adding materially to our knowledge of this ancient but interesting civilization.

MEXICAN MONEY.

BY STEIN.

The money of Mexico is nominally in *peso* (dollars) and *centavos* (cents); and the standard is what is termed a mixed one, gold and silver combined, as is that of the United States. Mexican gold, however, is rare money, difficult to obtain; and in exchange their twenty-dollar piece is not worth quite as much as our own "double eagle," though of exactly the same weight.

But one gets very little idea of the current names of coins and the common language of the people in buying and selling from consulting the written table of a nation's money

In a Mexican shop you hear nothing of *centavos* (cents). Ask the price of some small article, and you will very likely receive for answer, "*Un claco, señor.*"

A *claco* is an old copper coin worth a cent and a half. Or perhaps the shopman will say, *Cuatillo* (pronounced *quart-ee-yo*).

A *cuatillo* is two *elacos*. If the article is of rather greater value he may say, "*un medio,*" or perhaps "*un real.*"

A *medio* is a little silver coin worth six and a quarter cents; a *real* is twelve and a half cents, very like in size and value to an old English "ninepence."

AZTEC NUMBERS.

If you have survived the ordeal of a Mexican barber-shop, and arisen — unrecognizable to your dearest friends — from under the handiwork of a Mexican artist in *pelo-corta*, this gentleman will probably announce his fee to you as "*dos reales, señor,*" two reals, which is our twenty-five cents, or the "two bits" of the West.

Articles and fees of higher rate are commonly given as *tre' reales, cuatro reales, seis* or *sei'* (pronounced say) *reales, siete reales,* and so on, up to *veinte reales,* twenty reals; or perhaps *tres reales y medio,* or *cuatro reales y medio,* and the like, so on.

Practically silver is the standard of value in Mexico. The various *Nacional* and other *bancos* issue five, ten, twenty, and fifty dollar notes, which you may or may not find at a discount in the different States and cities. It is safer to take your money in silver dollars. But this — even if you have no more than one or two hundred dollars — is one of the burdens of life in Mexico. Two hundred dollars in silver weighs almost seventeen pounds, and if you are unlucky enough to have a thousand dollars your situation is, indeed, deplorable! You must watch it as never a cat watches a mouse, or it will be stolen; and on all the stage and railway lines they charge you from six to ten and twelve cents per kilogramme weight, till the pile dwindles away paying its own transportation. Yet no tourist must make the mistake of taking the paper bank-notes out of the country. These are practically worthless everywhere out of Mexico; and as for the Mexican silver dollars they are worth nominally, at present valuation, eighty-six cents each at exchange in New York and other larger cities in the United States, but no more than eighty cents if you have a few to pass in making small purchases. It is to be hoped that as trade and travel increases between the two republics some more convenient money medium may be devised.

TOUGH AS A BULL.

BY MOSES O.

"Tough as a bull" is a phrase which has passed into a proverb, the truth of which was well demonstrated by an incident which occurred a few weeks since on board the steamship "City of Merida," while lying off Progresso, the port of Merida, the capital of the Mexican State of Yucatan.

Progresso has no harbor. Vessels coming here have to anchor five or six miles off the coast, and transfer their freights to large "lighters," which put off to receive it. Even at this distance from shore there is not more than forty feet of water. These are the "grand banks" of Yucatan, where extensive fisheries are made.

There were on board the steamer two large, short-horn bulls, which the owner of a stock-range inland was importing at a considerable expense; one of them in particular was a very fine animal, weighing about two thousand pounds, round, well-knit, and of a "glossy, grizzle" color, with a few yellow-white patches on his sleek sides. All through the voyage we had been admiring him as he stood in his temporary stall in the forward hold, his feet set wide apart to brace himself against the rolling motion of the ship.

When the moment for disembarking him to the lighter came, the deck hands

— who, perhaps, stood a little in fear of him — passed a broad, stout canvas sling beneath his belly merely. Into this a tackle and block, descending from the yard and worked by the "pony" engine, was hooked, when presto! Mr. Taurus was run up through the hatchway, and in a moment hung suspended fifteen feet above the main deck, his eyes rolling in surly amazement at his sudden elevation and the wide expanse of sea and sky about him.

They then hooked another block into his sling in order to swing him off clear of the vessel, to lower him into the lighter, which lay alongside. But with the first pull on this second line the great animal's body, not being properly secured in the sling, slid out of it backwards and fell — turning a somersault as he went down — upon the outer verge of the deck, and thence bounded off, turning still another somersault, into the bottom of the lighter! — a distance of at least thirty-five feet.

The lighter shook!

"He's a dead bull!" "Must have broken every bone in him!" "He's burst!" were some of the exclamations that rose from all who saw the animal fall.

For a moment or two the big fellow lay quite still. One of the men threw a bucket of water over him, whereat he shook his head, and to the surprise of everybody, got up, gave his side a lash with his tail, and, stepping along to a bale of hay, began to help himself as if nothing of any consequence had happened.

Apparently he was unhurt; and whatever his opinion may have been of the clumsy way in which he was trans-shipped, he kept it contemptuously to himself.

THE CATHOLIC CHURCH IN MEXICO.

BY THE DIVINITY STUDENT.

THERE are in Mexico three thousand eight hundred and seventy-four Catholic churches and cathedrals, and scarcely more than six Protestant churches. Mexico may, therefore, be correctly regarded as a Catholic country, and, indeed, it would be difficult to over-estimate the influence of this Church with the common people.

It would be a great mistake, however, to suppose that the Church has any controlling influence in government affairs. In this respect Mexico is at present the most liberal country in the world. The former power of the Church

THE CHURCH.

has been absolutely nullified. Under the wise administration of Benito Juarez in 1867, all the property of the Church, to the amount of nigh three hundred million dollars, was "nationalized,"— confiscated for the use of the nation. All the churches and cathedrals are now the absolute property of the civil government, not of the Church; and the priests are merely tenants by courtesy of that government. Any or all these churches are liable at any moment to be taken possession of, and used for national purposes.

At the same time the Jesuits and several other ambitious Catholic societies were suppressed, and their *personnel* sent out of the country.

Religious processions and parades are strictly prohibited by law. Any priest appearing in the streets or anywhere out of the church edifice in his clerical robes is subject to fine and imprisonment.

Such a law seems arbitrary, but was necessary to prevent the absurd custom of the people kissing the hands of the priests in the streets. Twenty years ago it was common to see crowds of the peons paying a medio or a real for the privilege of kissing the padre's hand in the street. The liberal rulers of Mexico judged rightly that no proper self-respect could be engendered in a people when addicted to such abject practices.

MEXICAN PRIESTS OF THE PAST.

The civil officials register births, perform the marriage ceremony, and take charge of the burial of the dead. While it is not prohibited to the Church to marry, marriages may still be solemnized by a priest if the parties desire; but the ceremony has no validity. Civil marriages alone are legal.

These reforms are the hard-earned results of sixty years' warfare between the Church and the liberal progressive party in Mexico.

Under the brief reign of Maximilian the powers of the Church revived ; but with the final triumph of Juarez, in 1867, all the reform laws were put in rigid execution.

GENERAL PORFIRIO DIAZ.

There is an anecdote of Gen. Diaz, — the same who has of late made so brilliant a tour in the United States. While at one time a prisoner in the hands of the rival party, and confined in the rear of an old church, he was awakened from sleep at the dead of night by the presence of a priest in his dungeon.

"My son," said the ecclesiastic, "swear to me that you will reinstate the Church in her former powers, and I will set you at liberty this night, and the Holy Church shall support all your claims to authority.

Diaz was ambitious, but had no mind to owe his elevation to the Church.

"How have you entered my cell, padre?" he asked.

"By a secret passage leading from the church," was the reply.

"Surely, where you have come in, I can go out," exclaimed the future president ; and, bounding off his couch, he threw the priest on the floor, gagged him, and tied him hand and foot with his black robes, torn in strips. This done, he walked out and escaped.

Episodes like this illustrate, though but faintly, the long, bitter, and inveterate struggle between Church and State in Mexico.

CHAPTER XIV.

POPOCATAPETL. — A PERMIT TO ASCEND THE VOLCAN. — AMECAMECA. — THE VOLCANEROS. — GRAND VIEWS. — IXTACCIHUATL. — AT THE HALF-WAY RANCHO. — SULPHUR MOULDING. — A COLD NIGHT AND A FROSTY MORNING. — THE LINE OF ETERNAL SNOW. — IN THE BLACK SAND. — COLLAPSE OF MOSES AND THE SCRIBE — SNOW-BLIND. — VICTORY FOR A FEW. — THE TOP OF POPO. — THE CRATER. — "WE'VE CLIMBED IT." — FAREWELL TO MEXICO.

THOUGH we have no personal interest in recommending anybody's book, we venture to suggest to every young tourist to read — either on his voyage to Mexico, or immediately on his arrival in the country — Prescott's "Conquest of Mexico," and General Wallace's "Fair God." These books will make his visit signify a great deal more to him, and invest all the places and scenes, particularly those about the capital, with true classic interest.

Going out along the tranvia to Atzcapotzalco, we pass a large, gnarled old tree, inclosed by a railing. Ordinarily, it might attract no more than a passing notice; but our reading enabled us to identify it as the venerable tree beneath which Cortez sat after the memorable passage of the causeway, on the *noche triste*, when all seemed lost.

On the street leading out northwest from the Alameda, we pass a shop bearing as its sign the words, "Salto de Alvarado." Hard by is the place where, according to history, Alvarado made his wonderful leap for life, when pursued by the Aztecs along the causeway to the fatal gap of the drawbridge, where so many of his countrymen per-

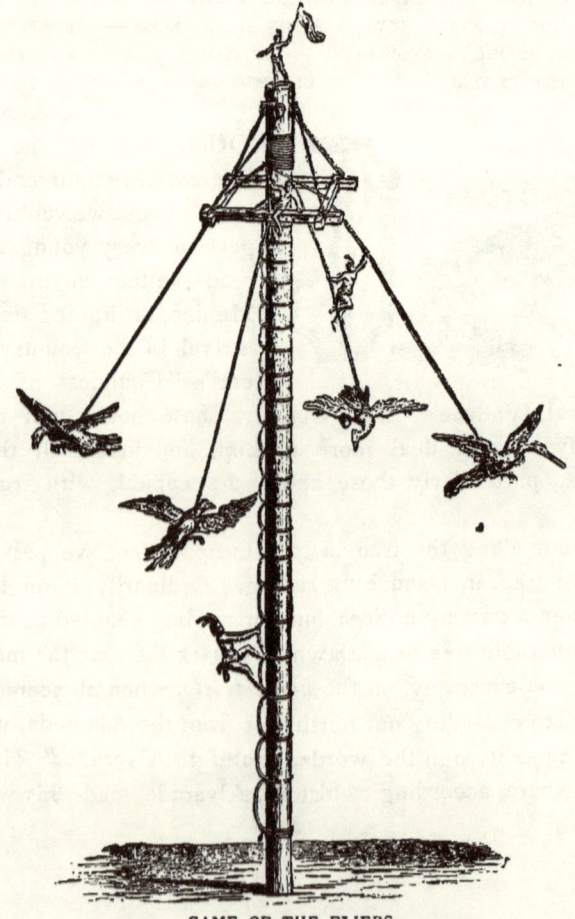

GAME OF THE FLIERS.

ished on the *noche triste*. And so of a score other places which the wonderful story of the past will illumine.

Our month in Mexico was drawing to a close; but ere setting off by rail and diligence for San Blas, on the Pacific coast, where we were to take the steamer for San Francisco, we determined to crown our visit by climbing Popocatapetl, the taller of the grand snow-clad volcanoes which tower on the southern rim of the valley. Toward these, morning and evening, the admiring, longing glances of several of our party had been directed, and at length a vote was obtained to attempt the ascent.

Popocatapetl has an owner. It is the property of the Mexican General Ochoa, who works the sulphur mines at the bottom of the crater, — for the destruction of his country's foes. It is necessary to have a permit from him to visit the summit. Our first application for one was not crowned with success, not from any lack of courtesy on the part of the general, but on account of the great quantity of snow on the mountain. He did not deem it safe for us to make the attempt, and we were refused a permit, solely for our own good. It was not easy to find fault with such a man. During all the first days of March the mountain was snow-clad for seven thousand feet downward from its summit; but soon after the 20th of the month the weather became warmer, and the snow-line retreated upward. In consequence of this change a permit was accorded us.

We were advised by some to go to Puebla, and make that place our point of departure for the mountain. Others assured us that Amecameca, a large village on the narrow-guage railway to Morelos, was the best place to ascend from. In some doubt, we chose the latter route; and, having mustered our party, and provided ourselves with what seemed a proper equipment in the way of heavy boots, old suits, iron-shod staves, green goggles, and weapons, we left the city at 7.30 in the morning, and reached Amecameca at 10.15.

We established ourselves for the day at the hotel and restaurant alongside of the station, and busied ourselves in bespeaking various volcaneros — men who work the sulphur mine in the crater of Popocatapetl — as guides for our proposed ascent next morning. At length we made a bargain with two brothers, named Ruiz, who were to furnish five peons and thirteen horses, in addition to their own services, for the sum of twenty dollars per day, be the trip longer or shorter. No one could find fault with such terms, particularly as they were to board themselves. The names of the brothers were

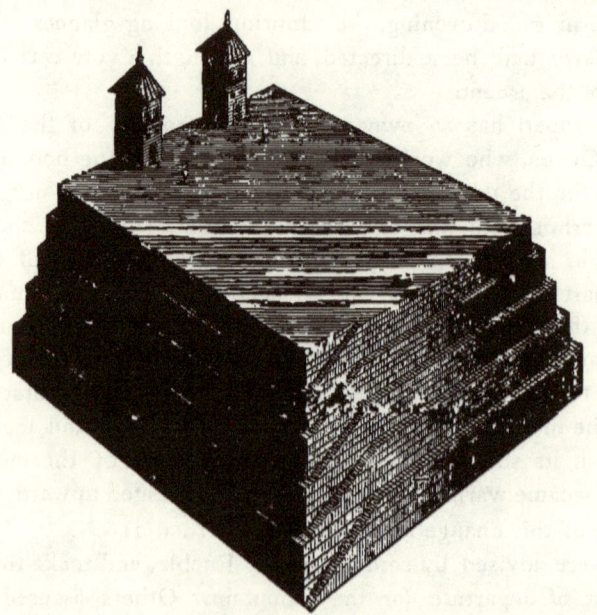

AN ANCIENT AZTEC TEOCELLI.

Manuel and Pedro; and among the peons, as we learned next day, there were two Josés, one José Maria (Mary Joseph), and a Jesus,— all young male Indians, dressed in white cotton and shod with open sandals. Jesus, in fact, is a very common given-name among these people. The pronunciation is Haysooz; and as it seems rather sacrilegious to northern ears to call a boy Jesus, we will speak of our peon as Haysooz.

It took a vast deal of bargaining to accomplish this arrangement; but we still had time left to lie for an hour in the shade of the grand old cedars at the foot of the Hill of the Sacrament, and watch the setting sun on the mountains. It had been very smoky during the forenoon, and clouds had at times obscured the white peaks; but toward sunset these were wafted away; and the golden light resting on the vast sheets of snow and ice created for us a scene so ethereally beautiful that we could scarcely believe it to be part and parcel of our commonplace old earth. But there were things at the "hotel" where we passed the night, both at our table and in our couches, which fully demonstrated that no spot on earth is perfect as yet. We need refer to them no further than to say that they materially assisted us to rise at an early hour. At five o'clock our entire party of nine young gentlemen were astir to a man. Coffee was taken, and everything in the way of equipments prepared. Mr. Brett had an aneroid barometer, and Forney undertook to carry up a thermometer; we affected nothing further in the line of scientific instruments. Altogether we had five repeating-carbines. Each man, too, had a revolver; and, being so large a party, we concluded that we could safely dispense with the services of a guard of soldiers, with which solitary tourists up the mountain are commonly provided as a protection against robbers and mountain-lions. And, indeed, the numerous black crosses along the various paths leading up the sides of Popocatepetl abundantly indicate that such a guard is necessary. Each of these funereal emblems marks the spot where some luckless pedestrian has been laid aside.

At length the horses — wiry little scrubs — and mules were mustered, and we mounted and set off from the hotel toward the mountain. The morning was delightfully fresh, as are all the mornings on the great plateau. For an hour we rode past fields of barley and maize, gradually ascending to the pines.

The Indian laborers were astir, trotting along their paths with their back-loads of jarras, fruit, and petate. Soon we began to meet mules, dragging sticks of timber down from the mountain. Instead of carts,

MONTEZUMA.

they here fasten a squared timber on each side of the animal, and allow the ends to drag on the ground.

The path taken by our guides presently grew steeper. We had frequent barrancas, or ravines, to cross, and for the next three or four hours worked our way steadily upward, not without some difficult riding for several of our party. The peons, bearing loads of provisions, overcoats, blankets, etc., followed on foot. As yet we experienced no difficulty of respiration on account of the height, which was already several thousand feet above sea-level.

At eleven o'clock we reached a rancho, which at present serves as a half-way house for tourists climbing the mountain. Formerly it was a stock-ranch, but now the buildings are used as a rude fabrica for subliming and molding sulphur brought down from the crater. They melt it in earthen jarras, which are broken from the sulphur cake when cool.

We had a letter from General Ochoa to the foreman, or majordomo, of the rancho; but we found no one about the premises except two peons, who could not read a word either in script or print. Our two guides explained to them the purport of the letter; and, although they were far from cordial, they did not withstand our taking possession of the casa, and making ourselves at home in it. The place is in a wooded valley, well up toward the limit of vegetation. Even at noon the air was cool and fresh. There is an ice-cold brook hard by. It is a good situation for a half-way house, though rather cold, as we began to feel by three in the afternoon.

There were barely accommodations for so large a party. In fact, there was but one bed, and that a strip of straw mat, nailed to a bedstead. This the balance of the party very magnanimously voted to the scribe and the cadet, both of whom were too bashful to decline. The others had the usual reward of self-sacrifice, and in this case slept on the floor of the rancho, with their saddles or overcoats for pillows.

The morning seemed like a December morning in a New England forest. All the trees were sparkling with frost; an inch or two of snow lay about, and to crown the resemblance wintry little chick-a-dees were hopping from twig to twig. Moses came out sneezing, and there was a chorus of nasal notes and coughing from the entire party.

By sunrise our coffee was prepared; and by seven the horses were saddled, and all was ready for the ascent of the great white cone, glimpses of which we could catch through the pines about the rancho.

Step by step our horses toiled upward through the pine woods. Another deep barranca was crossed with difficulty; and then emerging on a sudden from the gnarled scrub, we found ourselves at the foot of a vast bed of loose, black sand, which is said to have been ejected from the volcan during some pre-historic irruption. It lay on a slope nearly as steep as the ordinary gambrel-roof of a house, — steeper in fact, in many places, — and the feet of the horses sank into it to their fetlocks at each step. Worse still, they slid backwards in it at least two steps in three; and the lightness of the air adding to their other troubles, their distressed pantings soon became painful to hear. This anomalous sort of progress, too, was nearly as tiresome to us who rode. Moses, Brett, and the "Thelog" immediately dismounted and waded upward on foot; but the guides advised us all to ride, saying that we should have walking enough to do later.

The sand-beds may not have been much over a mile in width, but we were certainly two hours working our way up to the snow-drifts above them.

We had reached the snow-line. From this point the peak loomed a thousand metres or more above our heads; and the way was over and amongst huge snow-banks and icy rocks protruding through them. The horses could take us no further, and were led back down the sand-slope by one of the peons.

Thus far it had been riding, difficult riding truly, but still riding. Now began the actual climbing, — climbing through soft snow and over slippery rocks, sometimes at an angle of much more than forty-five degrees. We had hoped to find the snow hard, but it proved soft enough to slump in to one's knees, and it lay treacherously over chasms and holes. The worst element of the difficulty, however, was the dazzling, utterly blinding glare of the sun on the snow-banks. Our green and blue glasses afforded little amelioration, and by the time we had climbed eight or ten hundred feet the scribe, whose eyes are at no time the best, was seized with such excruciatingly sharp pains in the left temple as to be quite incapable of sight or further progress. Moses, too, was suddenly discovered to be bleeding from both his nose and ears, and a violent pain in the chest had nearly prostrated the "Theolog," who sat down panting and protesting that he could go no higher. The peon Haysooz had given out several hundred feet below, and with him Mary Joseph. The other, Josés, having his feet wrapped in strips of blanket, kept on with the guides.

The aneroid barometer now indicated an altitude of 15,760 feet above sea-level, and not far from 8,000 feet above the City of Mexico. The view from this point was grand, no doubt; but the scribe, for one, was quite unable to behold it, and, making a virtue of dire necessity, made his way down out of the snow, over the sand slope, to the rancho as best he could, followed by Moses, the "Theolog," and Karzy; also by Haysooz, Mary Joseph, and the limping José.

We, the party of the inglorious retreat, reached the rancho among the pines in the ravine at about one o'clock.

The others, the excelsior party, had meantime pressed on toward the summit.

At about three o'clock Harold came back to the rancho with the last one of the Josés, having, when near the rocky spur known as the Pico del Fraile, been seized by the same sharp, cramping pain in the chest which had disabled Mr. Garland.

Nothing was seen of the other four young gentlemen, however, till between seven and eight o'clock in the evening, when they came in jubilant, triumphant. They had done it! They had ascended Popocatapetl! They had stood on the rim of the crater, and smelled the brimstone! They had heard the roar of the great subterranean fire-box! They had seen all Mexico lying outspread like a map at their feet.

Thus to us, the dejected ones, they held forth.

"The crater," said Stein, in reply to a timid question by the scribe, "is a semi-circular pit, with almost perpendicular inner walls at the very apex of the cone. It is about twelve hundred metres across the top, and from four to five hundred metres in depth. It smokes steadily sulphur fumes; it is these fumes, sublimed on the rocks at the bottom of the crater, which make the deposit worked by the volcaneros as a mine."

Mr. Brett reports the height of Popocatapetl, as indicated by the aneroid barometer, at 17,876 feet.

"Well," said Moses, when this much of information had been elicited, "we've climbed it, — not all of us, individually, but the party — our party — has climbed it. More we cannot boast to-day."

And thus — not altogether triumphantly, nor yet ignominiously — terminated our experience of Popocatapetl.

www.ingramcontent.com/pod-product-compliance
Lightning Source LLC
Chambersburg PA
CBHW021809230426
43669CB00008B/682